AF321477

Judgment and Contemporary Art Criticism

Judgment and Contemporary Art Criticism

Edited by Jeff Khonsary & Melanie O'Brian
Artspeak / Fillip Editions 2010

Folio Series: A

Contents

Over the past decade, we have seen remarkable levels of market speculation and investment in contemporary art while world economies find themselves on uncertain ground. Concurrently, there has been a new wave of interest in the efficacy and function of art criticism focused on the role of judgment and valuation in contemporary art writing. Yet while the economy of contemporary art seems to demand rigorous critique, art writing often functions solely in the service of an expanding, unregulated art market. It was in the context of this conflicted set of concerns that, in February 2009, Artspeak and Fillip presented *Judgment and Contemporary Art Criticism*, a forum that laid the groundwork for this publication. Organized in conjunction with a reading room and discussion series held at Artspeak, the forum sought to offer a space to trouble the so-called crisis plaguing discourse around contemporary art criticism by deferring the question of art criticism's pending doom in favour of a discussion that stressed pragmatics over sensationalism and morbidity.

For many, the end of the twentieth century witnessed a mitigation of the importance of critical judgment initially established by Enlightenment principles and strengthened within high modernist discourses. Described by critic James Elkins as "one of the most significant changes in the art world in the previous century,"[1] this "ebb of judgment" developed out of a larger poststructuralist project that actively resisted the ostensibly closed space of individual valuation. Instead, many critics argued for a more open dialogue between texts and objects, pursuing modes of critique that allowed for the exploration of ambiguity and interpretation, thus detaching art writing from questions of quality.

Yet with the start of the new millennium, a growing chorus of critics have begun declaring the failure of interpretation in the absence of evaluative criticism. As Christopher Bedford, editor of *X-TRA* magazine, argues: "Most vitally for me as a critic, informed judgment predicated on explicitly stated, clearly enumerated criteria represents the foundation for the most advanced, productive critical discourse."[2] Developed in tandem with anxiety over a looming crisis in the profession and the increasing prevalence of descriptive reportage, this position stresses that a return to qualitative judgment is a remedy to the cauterized state of contemporary art criticism.

Addressing this growing tension, the present project attempts to provide a space in which to discuss the prospect of critical valuation beyond questions of professional binaries. The questions we posed included: Can judgment operate within new modalities of writing that hold open a reflexive space for ambiguity and dialogue? How would these new forms read? What is the ongoing significance of more "traditional" forms of writing, such as the review? If, as Boris Groys has claimed, critical discourse today is an attempt to "bridge the divide" between the "inherited older public office" of the critic who judged art "in the name of the public" and the "avant-garde's betrayal of this office," can new forms of criticism remake judgment anew, without making explicit determinations of quality?[3]

It was with a longstanding interest in these questions that we developed the *Judgment and Contemporary Art Criticism* forum. Held over two days at Emily Carr University, the forum was contextualized by a supplementary reader featuring reprints of key texts on art criticism and valuation distributed prior to the event. The forum began with a keynote paper by Tirdad Zolghadr that assessed current discussions around art criticism through a what he identified as schematic, three-step process: a definition of a crisis within the field, a call to order, and a moment in which common ground is sought between the two. The first panel, addressing the critical space of the art review, featured papers by Tom Morton, William Wood, and Kristina Lee Podesva, and was moderated by John O'Brian. The second panel, examining valuation in more genre-blurred forms of art criticism, included papers by Diedrich Diederichsen and Maria Fusco and was moderated by Jeff Derksen. This forum was complemented by a month-long discussion series held at the reading room in Artspeak's exhibition space. Events included a talk by architect/writer Markus Miessen, a video conference with critic Sven Lütticken, an interview between curator and writer Jo-Anne Birnie-Danzker and Jordan Strom, and a screening of the film *A Crime Against Art* (Hila Peleg, 2007).

This volume presents papers developed out of the two-day forum and an excerpt of transcripts from the public discussion during the question periods.[4] These texts are complemented by essays by Sven Lütticken and James Elkins, who were asked to participate in the discussion as respondents. Lütticken's and Elkins's analyses of the field of art criticism were central to our own internal discussions of the field as this project developed, and their inclusion here provides an important addition to the discourse. Vancouver itself is an important context for the debates that have developed during this series of events. Over the last several decades, significant public conversations in the city developed parallel to discussions of critical art writing, but no formal consideration of the field of criticism itself emerged.[5] Central to our project, therefore, was an effort to develop a conversation that engaged both international *and* local critics and artists in a discussion of contemporary criticism. Although the city is positioned at a geographic periphery, Vancouver's cultural identity has evolved in tandem with debates and concerns influencing international contemporary art. This dialogue emerged through interactions with visiting artists, writers, and curators throughout the late 1960s and early 1970s—a moment when conceptual art and the spread of independent publishing and writing created new possibilities for a decentralized critical art community.[6] It is Vancouver's longstanding connection to an international critical community that provides the conditions within which Artspeak and Fillip operate.

The concerns of the present volume have been central to Fillip's own development. Through an active publishing and event program, Fillip scrutinizes the form, function, and efficacy of critical discourses around art. Like Fillip, Artspeak provides a space for extended dialogue between visual art and language. Since 1986, Artspeak has published critical writing within the context of contemporary art, from belle lettrist, parallel texts, and ficto-criticism to descriptive and cultural commentary, as well as ongoing public discourse and conversation. The *Judgment and Contemporary Art Criticism* project constitutes a significant, rather than a definitive, contribution to an ongoing international discussion regarding the role of criticism in a rapidly changing art system.

This project would not have been possible without the help and support of a number of individuals and organizations, foremost the writers and participants in the forum and subsequent discussion sessions: Jo-Anne Birnie-Danzker, Jeff Derksen, Diedrich Diederichsen, James Elkins, Maria Fusco, Sven Lütticken, Markus Miessen, Tom

Morton, John O'Brian, Kristina Lee Podesva, William Wood, and Tirdad Zolghadr. Particular thanks are due to Jordan Strom, who was crucial in the conceptualization of the structure and focus of the forum, and without whom this project would not have begun. Additional thanks to Meredith Carr, Peter Gazendam, Jonathan Middleton, Kate Steinmann, and Amy Zion for the countless hours they spent in support of this endeavor.

This publication has been made possible through the specific support of the British Columbia Arts Council's Special Project Assistance Unique Opportunities. The forum was presented with the Vancouver 2009 Cultural Olympiad, with additional support provided by the British Columbia Arts Council's Special Project Assistance Unique Opportunities. The keynote paper received support from the Emily Carr University speaker series. Both Fillip and Artspeak would like to acknowledge the ongoing support received from The Canada Council for the Arts and the British Columbia Arts Council. Artspeak acknowledges the additional support of the City of Vancouver.

– Jeff Khonsary and Melanie O'Brian

1. James Elkins, *What Happened to Art Criticism?* (Chicago: Prickly Paradigm Press, 2003), 48.
2. Christopher Bedford, "Art Without Criticism," *X-TRA* 10, no. 2 (winter 2007), 7.
3. Boris Groys, "Critical Reflections," in *The State of Art Criticism*, Michael Newman and James Elkins, eds. (New York: Routledge, 2007), 63.
4. Those interested in hearing the original talks are encouraged to visit the Fillip Web site, where they are available in

an audio podcast. See http://fillip.ca.

5. Clement Greenberg and T. J. Clark visited the University of British Columbia in 1981 for the conference *Modernism and Modernity: A Question of Culture, or Culture Called into Question*. Stan Douglas organized a public series of talks in 1990 that led to *Vancouver Anthology: The Institutional Politics of Art* (Vancouver: Or Gallery and Talonbooks, 1991), which was followed by Artspeak's reconsideration of how a local art history is articulated in this city in the forum and publication *Vancouver Art and Economies* (Vancouver: Arsenal Pulp Press and Artspeak, 2007).

6. Lucy Lippard, *Six Years: The Dematerialization of the Art Object From 1966 to 1972* (Berkeley: University of California Press, 1973), xviii.

Tirdad Zolghadr
Worse than Kenosis

The *Judgment and Contemporary Art Criticism* forum pitted an unnamed set of "judges" against an intellectual generation with a strong ideological sympathy for "criticality" in art. In my keynote address, I made a stand for the latter that surprised even me in its resolve, fussily rejecting the idea of judgment in favor of self-reflexivity, persistent recontextualization, and so on. In place of judgment, I proposed the rehabilitation of notions of professional specificity. By the end of the forum, I was not so sure about this assertion. Contributions like my own, which advocated some free flow of post-factual ambivalence, seemed a little too nice, even self-congratulatory, in that fair-trade sun-dried-tomatoes kind of way. Clever, in the worst sense of the term. A position like Diedrich Diederichsen's, by contrast—a persuasive plea for judgment as both inevitable and invigorating—seemed the reasonable way to go. A good old T-bone steak. To make things worse, Diederichsen was backed up by audience member Stan Douglas, who referred to Theodor Adorno's mildly racist indictment of jazz to say: at least the guy had a position. Judgment, in this context, amounts to robust opinions asserting what is good, bad, or ugly, according to clearly voiced criteria, which is hoped to offer more transparency both in terms of the writers' positions and in terms of characterizing the art that is being debated.

It wasn't easy, but I've reconsidered. I've decided Diederichsen, Douglas, and Adorno can judge all they like. As long as the field is littered with professionals even half as perceptive. Judgment needs a critical ethos beyond a friendly set of advisory checks and balances. It needs to be repeatedly deconstructed from within. If you trace the matter closely enough, within the confines of the existing contemporary art field, you begin to notice that most things judgmental have a pointed tendency to be pointlessly injurious, pointlessly embarrassing, or both. You have newspaper critics offering unmitigated gut reactions to, say, the Turner Prize shortlist, as if their raw innards held precious gems of ideological truth: *The frontrunner leaves me cold. He has never done more than mildly irritate me.* Gut feeling is posited as the more "honest" source of insight. You have academy teachers with authoritarian aplomb encouraging impulsive judgment in their students, at the expense of prolonged self-criticism. You have curators in the Middle East making blanket evaluations that afford them an aura of spokesmanship and sometimes wanton political power. Inevitable? Perhaps. But advisable, useful, critical?

Dialectics

Since this book is critiquing critics and judging judges, I'll begin with a comment that is modest but clearly prescriptive. I appreciate art writing that is specific in that it starts with the material. Not the art, necessarily, but the material format that supports the critical event in itself, be it situational, infrastructural, or such. This is why I tend to start with the premise of the current volume. After which I shall offer my own idea of a crisis, an alternative to the one sketched out in the forum's original brief. Crisis is widely seen as a dialectical lubricant, moving things along from one stage of stability to the next, and in many contexts that is a reasonable definition, surely. But in a setting such as criticism, crisis needs to be addressed first and foremost as a constant companion, a trope that is conjured, more or less dramatically, more or less explicitly, as an inevitable

step in the critical process. Crisis not as an exceptional di-
saster zone, but as a stabilizing, homeopathic cough drop.
Following all this, I'll finally pitch a few unexceptional,
moderate ideas about directions to consider. The ideas are
unexceptional and moderate in that they amount to little
more than a circumscription of the distinctive features of
the field under scrutiny. This in itself, I'd like to argue, is a
step in a good direction.

Before we get to the material format of the brief that
framed the forum from which this book has been produced,
consider, if you will, the format of the exhibition review.
The review is by now the most musty of master forms, the
oil painting of art writing. The difference being that oil
painting, much like stage theatre, has long come to terms
with its anachronisms and often succeeds in making virtue
out of necessity with self-reflexive verve. Reviews are about
as reflexive as West End Samuel Beckett reruns or art bien-
nials. Experimentation in content and ambition in form is
encouraged only within the confines of the classroom or
the hyperspecialized zine/journal, where it often becomes
extremely affected and slightly boring. In the more influ-
ential art magazine arena, on the other hand, reviews are
not only pedestrian, they are also deeply descriptive in
character. A 2002 Columbia University survey[1] showed a
comfortable majority of critics saw their work as a matter of description first and foremost (interestingly, "judging
art" was regarded the least popular activity). This is hardly
surprising given that most of today's reviews are as illustra-
tive and explanatory as they were two centuries ago, when
installation images were scarce and reviews were thus un-
adulterated *ekphrasis*.

But at least the review is recognized as a critical genre.
The conference brief, by contrast, goes unnoticed and un-
theorized. Conference briefs are aggressively prescriptive,

often drastically reining in the speaker's intentions, and yet they are carelessly discarded in cabs and bus shelters after lying folded up in our Wranglers. In this, the brief is similar to exhibition press statements and vernissage gossip blogs. Rarely mentioned in analytical settings, they are potent, volatile, and overwhelming when left unchecked, like heroin or swine flu or any matter that is left to fend for itself. Sometimes, they are mistakenly considered harmless due to their lack of narrative specificity. Indeed, they often render the issues obscure, like the near-proverbial rhetorical spin cycle on the curatorial washing machine: *Which are the key criteria underlying decision-making processes in the competitive struggle for public attention in the arts and the creative industries, and, moreover, in this context, what is the precise function of immaterial goods such as "authenticity," "originality" and the like, etc.?* On the other hand, when they are more specific, they're utterly unrealistic in timing: *Each of you has ten minutes to make a statement on the current state of art criticism, art magazines, the relationship between the art critic and curator, how contemporary theory and politics feed into curatorial practice, etc.* But influence does not depend on narrative specificity or on well-timed logistics. One of the accusations criticality is facing is that its dense, ambiguous rhetoric makes it precisely less vulnerable. The *Judgment and Contemporary Art Criticism* brief avoided these pitfalls. The title is refreshingly deadpan and unassuming. A relief from necrophiliac proclamations of the demise of the public, the death of the critic, the devastation of humankind, and this and that.

The e-mail brief sent out to the conference participants prior to the event argued that twentieth-century "mitigation of the importance of critical valuation established within high modernist discourses" led to many critics arguing for a more open "dialogue between texts and objects."

More recently, however, a growing chorus of critics began to argue that "a return to judgment was a remedy to the cauterized state of contemporary art criticism." The question is, therefore: "Can judgment operate within new modalities of writing that hold open a reflexive space for ambiguity and dialogue?"

There is more drama to come. The context is defined as "unbridled art market speculation in parallel with war and economic collapse." Whether one has spawned the other, or whether they all suffer from similar causes, is unclear. But the organizers ostensibly provide the backdrop for the question of function and efficacy of contemporary art writing. Surprisingly, the invasion of Afghanistan, the collapse of financial markets, and the inflated price of a Peter Doig are indeed related, be it only in their implications for the efficacy and perceived agency of art writing. The common denominator here is a perpetually frustrated appetite for consequentiality on writers' behalf, the shameful suspicion that the symbolic is not enough in a setting as volatile and violent.

Shame, as Karl Marx would have it, is an underrated revolutionary sentiment. But if we agree that shame is not an option, that a more dignified response is expected at a professional conference, perhaps the most optimistic way to frame agency within criticism and to posit writing as an actual high ground of agency is to evoke the comic strip division of labour between word and image and to argue that word is to image as speech is to action or thought is to bodies. This is to imply that we intervene in the overall distribution of forms of visibility, that we put things on the map. And in this, ours is not fundamentally different from internationalist humanitarian efforts, seeing as, after all, even the UN draws attention to crises—in a manner that disregards boundaries between institutions, disciplines, nation states—as a central part of its mission. Others have argued that inefficacy is not the problem, so much as is the shame in it, precisely. One might embrace the inefficacy instead. Perform the marginality and espouse the latency in the hope of construing pockets of ambiguity in a mass culture of high performance. The idea of kenosis—self-emptying in the spirit of openness to signals from above—is as old as the hills. As the tastefully ambiguous, the strategically latent, and the otherwise marginal have liked to point out since Aristotle, the highest form of power is actually the power not to act. The conference brief names a third possibility of reacting to the crisis of inefficacy: "value and judgment are returning to the forefront of debates about the social function of the art critic." Beyond Rancièreian regimes of visibility and *Bartleby the Scrivener*, we have the Tough Love approach. *Someone's gotta sweep them streets.* Setting aside the content for a moment, it is undeniable that the dialectic at hand is a familiar structural ruse.

Thesis: a theory-driven practice of metacommentary strives to do justice to a shifting, heterogeneous public, to the very dialogue unfolding between texts and their objects, leading to a rigorous detachment from questions of quality towards questions of context, ideology, etc.—a shift Irit Rogoff has successfully summarized as moving from criticism to critique to criticality.[2] From finding fault to tracing tacit assumptions that make something seem persuasive to observing from an ambivalent ground that builds on both earlier moments but also wishes to acknowledge the speaker's own complicities. "This show is bullshit" becomes, "What do I mean by *show*, by *is*, and by *bullshit*?" To eventually become, "How am I consolidating those notions by virtue of the very fact of discussing them, and I should be noting how people are dressed at the opening? Maybe that's more important than the bullshit."

The above process is, of course, easily parodied as affected and pompous. Even precious allies such as Terry Eagleton gleefully describe a post-60s generation heroically moving from "what is going on" to "what the fuck's all this," only to land in theoretically buttressed, stylish bewilderment. Nothing is more voguish in guilt-ridden Anglo-American academia, he argues, than to point to the inevitable bad faith of one's position. It's the nearest, Eagleton quips, that a postmodernist can come to authenticity.[3]

The suspicion here is that frictionless thoughtfulness is bad for agency. But also that it invigorates free market ideology. Or, in other words, that the death of the critic does not spawn the birth of the emancipated reader so much as that of the consumer, the nonchalance of "can't everyone just do what they want." In many ways, this is undeniable. In the present-day art context, a writer like, say, Alain Badiou is instrumentalized not to undermine categories of understanding in any rigorously uncomfortable manner, but in the way Vodafone marketing might tap into our appetite for something wild. Being critical means being radically open, non-committal, because new truths may strike at any time, a notion of epistemic flow that anyone from Vodafone marketing to Nicolas Bourriaud to the Israeli Defence Forces would subscribe to. How, critics rightly ask, can this temperament be helpful in a context of post-Fordist conditions of production, where professional uncertainty, apprehension, and interruption is to be welcomed as good, clean, crazy fun?

This complicity has been tracked down even deeper within the preferred modus of experimental art writing, the "essayistic," by which I mean a preference for the formally light-footed, the associative, the brief and passing, over the well-referenced, commanding hypothesis. Artist Hito Steyerl, in her collection of essays *Die Farbe der Wahrheit*, describes Adorno's *laudatiae* for these playful "rebellions against identity" and agrees that the essayistic is liberated from "the guild-like interdependencies of the academy and its systematic reproduction of its own class- and power-relationships. Since it is forced to communicate in constantly new contexts, its language is accessible, associative, and steers clear of jargons and quotation cartels."[4] But she's quick to add that the *Kraft der Unterbrechung*, the freestyle staccato of essayism, also reflects the project-to-project goose chase that is part and parcel of latter-day professionalism. Aside from being rebellious against intellectualized identity, typical art writing seamlessly integrates the interruptions of post-Fordist rhythm into its form.

And yet, who is to say that more clear-cut forms of judgment do not go down well in a context of ferocious market pressures? Consider the mounting pressure in art schools and institutions across the world to produce "results," to "engage with wider audiences," to offer something visible, tangible, unambiguous. If anything, at the end of the day, the modesty of persistent self-reflexivity looks decidedly less marketable than the controversy of stolid black and white. If you won't take it from an art writer, ask any museum director, or any artist, for that matter.

Moreover, there is a tremendous demand for any criteria (the starker and clearer the better) that might patch up the critical conundrum introduced by the internationalization of the contemporary art field when, in point of fact, criticality emerged with the realization that a strong dose of prudence, if not modesty, is appropriate when it comes to the convoluted critical discussions in a rapidly globalizing milieu.

Let's assume *Fillip* commissions a critical review of a video installation in Tehran. If the work is contextualized within a Tehran setting the audience is unfamiliar with, we risk instrumentalizing the art as an ethnographic return to the referent, an explanation or illustration of social realities. If, on the other hand, the review omits a rigorous description of the work's surroundings, we run the risk of a formalist exercise, defining the installation as a work from nowhere, bereft of sociopolitical setting. In the worst case, which is what usually occurs, the writer, well intended, opts for a little bit of both, with just enough contextual information to render the work a faraway fetish, but not enough to preclude the audience's wildest fantasies. The kind of contemporary art that is at stake in our field, in this book, and in this very essay, cannot possibly unfold without a reasonable amount of epistemic violence. The colonial subtext of the international contemporary art project is embarrassing and hard to raise, let alone theorize, no matter how much we believe in reinscription and appropriation and such. At the risk of sounding dramatic, reaching out, in a context of contemporary imperialism, will always also be a form of reining in.

So a good approach, possibly, would be to acknowledge that there is no possible reconciliation here, no moment of healing to be found, and to repeatedly bring the irresolvable contradictions to the fore. Things are all the more convoluted due to the fact that the internationalist agenda has long become a striking example of metalepsis, or a "metonymy of a metonymy."[5] We assume our cosmopolitan convictions compel us to travel and network across the Atlantic and beyond, when it's undeniably a mix of professional pressures and basic wanderlust that is the driving force here. In other words, internationalism, far from being a quasi-socialist means to a new society, has become a tautological end in itself, but still lends us the sprinkle of agency we crave. *Summa summarum*, in a muddled situation such as this, so perfectly rife for an abuse of power of exceptional proportions, the conceit of judgment will make things only worse. There's worse than kenosis.

To move on to the synthesis as defined by the brief, the antithesis naturally holds within itself the seeds of sublation. Rather than invoke a critical fashion police in Kantian knee stockings or Greenbergian corduroy, the forum brief asks us to consider whether synthesis is possible. A little bit of judgment, a little bit of kenosis, a little bit of autonomy, a little bit of authorship, a little bit of avant-garde. Of course it sounds like I'm being disrespectful, which is why I must clarify that Frankfurt Light, or Adorno Zero, really is what is proposed by my favorite art writers these days. It's a logical, tempting, and perfectly reasonable reaction. But it's based on a dialectic that is autogenerative and self-fulfilling and that says little about the empirical realities of judgment as critical practice.

It does, however, exemplify how the Hegelian foxtrot, one-two-three one-two-three, is constitutive of art writing. A definition of crisis within the field, a description of a nostalgic call to arms, and the conciliatory search for common-sensical middle ground. The thing about these teleological trinities is the fact that it always seems like we *had* to come to this conclusion. ABC, one-two-three. Dialectics offers rhyme and reason to wanton frictions, with the terms redistributed along an axis of opposition that is always already hierarchically oriented, so that the outcome of the tension is decided as soon as the opposition is identified.

Today, crises such as the one at stake in this very discussion hold strong geopolitical stakes, married, as they are, to the notion of radical pluralism marking a definitive stage in history, thereby marking in turn the supreme position of the West in the grander scheme of things. The idea of crisis here is a self-congratulating one. We've reached a stage of such utter democracy, pluralism, critical hubbub, it's starting to get annoying.

The one most elegant description of the central role of crises in the self image of the critical profession is arguably Paul de Man's "Criticism and Crisis," where we can see "the incredible swiftness with which tendencies succeed each other"[6] already being bemoaned in the nineteenth century. "Crisis" famously shares a common etymology with "criticism," and without crisis, de Man famously quipped, there is no criticism. Without crisis we can have philology, history, and many other things, but no criticism, because criticism is always comparing a given standard with a better one, in a better time or place. According to some, genuine criticism occurs only when it brings something to crisis, as opposed to when it fixes one, which sounds reasonable, but I would add that it would require a particular kind of crisis—not the kind we can happily agree on over dinner and some Hegel.

Crisis

Thankfully, language has a tendency to disassemble any object it attempts to police. A Florida ordinance against mooning defines buttocks in the following terms: *The area at the rear of the human body which lies between two imaginary lines running parallel to the ground when a person is standing—the first or top of such line drawn at the top of the cleavage of the nates (i.e. the prominence formed by the muscles running from the back of the hip to the back of the leg) and the second or bottom line drawn at the lowest visible point of this cleavage or the lowest point of the curvature of the fleshy protruberance, whichever is lower, and—between two imaginary lines on each side of the body, which run perpendicular to the ground and to the horizontal lines described above, and which perpendicular lines are drawn through the point at which each nate meets the outer side of each leg.*[7]

Language is a very bad tool with which to introduce the stringency of clear definition, as language will only ever lead to more language, and so, much like theses and antitheses themselves, the ethos of judgment holds the seeds of its own surpassing within it.

But what if we tweaked the definition of a crisis rather than rejecting it outright? As a friend of mine likes to say, "A couple of dilemmas and you have yourself a crisis." Which dilemma, then, might conjure a healthy crisis that need not partake in the dialectical bemoaning of Too Much Criticality? One such dilemma may be the question of how to define, and thus more precisely discuss, the activity of the critic without unnecessary limitations being imposed. The attraction of judgment also bespeaks a return to the moment when the function and the persona of the critic were crystal clear—a reaction to the loss of professional specificity that emerged with criticality's inherent bias toward radical interdisciplinarity, at the expense of clear art historical standards and institutionalized method.

It seems the art-critical insistence on epistemic *carte blanche* has borrowed heavily from the artistic side of things, from the artist's license, now more or less a century old, to colonize academic, architectural, activist, and televisual traditions with impunity. It is further buttressed by a formidable intellectual tradition ranging from Friedrich Nietzsche's "gay science" to the now established poststructuralist *doxa* of the 1970s and 80s to Bruno Latour's recent affirmations that our intellectual life is out of kilter, this being a hallmark setting us apart from pre-postmodern societies. We also have a range of curatorial approaches of comparable bent, from Sarat Maharaj's "xenoepisteme" to Irit Rogoff's "smuggling." Coming from a background in comparative literature, I know the benefits of this transdisciplinary culture very well, but I cannot help but notice there is indeed a dicey dilemma at hand. Because whenever critics, curators, and artists fail to be rigorously circumspect, they end up aping other traditions—emulating genealogies that are architectural, televisual, activist, and academic, all of which have far clearer sense of purpose than the arts. Finally, and most importantly, if the world is the art field's xenoepistemic oyster, then there's no place where it can be expected to sit down and shut up. This is not a good thing—particularly in the internationalized context I've been describing above.

Specificity

All of this leads me to propose not a rehabilitation of judgment but merely a stronger sense of critical specificity, a strategic essentialism to challenge the comfortable professional hybridizations that have become the rule: writer/researcher, critic/journalist, critic/editor, critic/curator, critic/journalist/editor/curator, critic/artist, writer/artist, etc. Not in the aim of constructing an empirical referent that lives up to conceptual purity of some sort, but to trace—and perhaps encourage—a particular atmosphere that pervades the room when you use the term "criticism." Teaching at the Center for Curatorial Studies at Bard College, I have been pursuing a similar discussion when it comes to curating, and it hasn't harmed anyone yet. On the contrary, this may be a modest alternative to the sublimating synthesis of "judgment plus ambiguity": "a definition of art writing, minus method and canonization." Specificity = definition − (method + canon). Can we have specificity without being the pompous old cretins in corduroy that Rogoff, Maharaj, and many others have worked hard to put back in their place?

To begin with, we have the issue of crisis itself. The ancient Greek *krisis* refered to a turning point in a disease. At the same time, *krinein* actually does mean "to judge," which confirms that judgment and crisis are, surely enough, part and parcel of one and the same deal. Crisis is undeniably the etymological mascot of the profession. Just as curators are endlessly reminded of the fact that their professional ancestors were the custodians of churches or, initially, the mentally disabled, the critic will have to listen to the occasional smartass quoting Paul de Man and ety-monline.com, so I'll give it a rest. Criticism also has its own specific histories, both canonical and subjugated, including a history of public roles and reputations. As significant as these genealogies are in this context, I don't think I need to go through them now. Instead, I'll offer a brief laundry list of four tenets the critic is (ostensibly and intrinsically) bound to. Tenets that may be worth revisiting, maybe not.

1. *Criticism is Critical* The *a priori* announcement that you're "critical" is usually self-emasculating, like calling yourself "rebellious" (or announcing how funny the joke is going to be). It evokes the idea of criticism as a contrapuntal reflex: once the critical becomes a principle, one's own position is not a position, really, but the mirror image of whoever is vis-à-vis yourself. The critical imperative also implies a restrictive chronological marching order. Critics react. They are not proactive or preemptive. You may have some who are ambitious enough to think curating, or art practices, can temporarily create a small movement, a fleeting scandal, or a specialized public. You will rarely hear that about criticism. Even Eagleton, diehard campaigner-zealot *par excellence*, argues that true criticism cannot fully exist until socialism has come into being and that this cannot be

the result of just criticism itself. Criticism, he mumbles in the melancholic conclusion of *The Function of Criticism*, is thus intrinsically condemned to wait.[8] The idea of the critic as "always too late" and similarly contrapuntal, deconstructive positions are of course simpatico. Perpetually rendering visible the mechanisms of political preconception, intellectualized laziness, institutionalized superstitions. But there's more to it, surely. The one most productive merging of critic and crisis lies in the idea of critics not shoring up crises and restoring law and order, but bringing things to crisis precisely by trying to deepen or enrich the crisis to the best of their abilities. This is not necessarily the same as being critical. If it's related to the critical, it's a distant cousin who is less noble, less refined, and less predictable.

2. *Criticism has an Audience* Art criticism beyond the newspaper barely has an audience at all. No one has taken this to a more rational conclusion, and with as much boyish candor, as Boris Groys, with his notion of "textual bikinis." A critical art text is not necessarily meant to be read, he suggests. Rather, it is there to avoid the embarrassment of discursive nudity.[9] Which is no cause for concern. The failure to communicate beyond a tiny specialized professional field is a liberating blessing—no promises made, none broken. Think of academia, with its countless books with no audience, their importance depending only on publication lists that prove to the respective patrons and benefactors that cultural capital is accumulating. If the pseudo-universal audience was finally banished from the art writing equation, then the peer group could be taken into account with more rigor. This brings me to a third tenet.

3. *Critics are Individuals* Critics are expected to be loners. Criticism is written individually, through a single fountainhead of analytical acumen. Unlike artists and curators, art writers do not have a peer group. No network

or socio-professional alliance to help them along. This precludes all sorts of collaborative possibilities that might make criticism a less predictable, more vibrant thing. A place where the aforementioned professional hybridities could come to the fore in the shape of variable, supple give and takes. Another disadvantage is tied to the work ethic. With such rigidly individualistic premises, post-Fordist conditions of production can only worsen. Critics rarely have much leeway beyond the usual shades of servile virtuosity, the most humiliating manifestation of which is the catalogue essay: the one well-paid commission critics can hope for is the one where they're paid to smile.

4. *Critics Use Language* As analyzed by W. J. T. Mitchell throughout his body of work, most famously in *Picture Theory: Essays on Verbal and Visual Representation* (1994), art criticism is indeed hopelessly indebted to language and the broader heritage of literary studies. Rather than complain about denegation, I prefer to suggest we live up to the resulting scopophobia with pride. The visual in visual art needn't be the teleological be-all end-all for the writer, but a pretext or camouflage, like calling something a sculpture park when it's more of a drinking corner, or a pork barrel. *Ekphrasis* doesn't do anyone any favours, least of all the artists. Personally, I now read reviews only of shows I've already seen. It's not that can you measure your opinion with that of the reviewer, but you get the most out of efforts made to see a show. More return on investment. Also, there is little point in writerly precision, textual verisimilitude, when art writing and art do not pursue the same agenda aesthetically or professionally.

This is already noticeable in the respective labour markets. If once there was a surplus of text with respect to image, at present, artists are writing their own commentaries, not because their agendas have merged, but because of a shortage of Groysian bikinis. A second way in which the critic momentarily has an edge over the artist is in that the former runs far less risk. Critics cannot err, seeing as, in the worst case, no one reads their work, and in the best case, the text functions much like a horoscope, wielding the graceful magic of self-fulfilling prophecy. If *Fillip* publishes a critique of the grizzly bear, chances are bears will not alter their behavior in any noticeable manner. But the said text on the hypothetical video installation in Tehran may have a considerable impact.

The lazy, easy, predictable way out is to simply play up the inherently ambivalent nature of language. Consider what critic/curator Polly Staple and I have termed "binary fluffing": the wanton pairing of vaguely incompatible terms to achieve poetic effect in a review.[10] Comically serious, playfully sincere, pleasantly troubling, obscurely illuminating. *John Smith's work is poetic and deadpan, enjoyably disturbing, high and low. It calls into question the way we create meaning. His work eludes categorization. His carefully selected objects are both specific and generic, metaphorical and actual. All of which goes well beyond questions of style*. Consider Rogoff hailing the "theorist undone by theory," or Liam Gillick talking of "unproductive factories" and "research without experimentation." But also the widespread Rancièrian notions of the "artwork as monument to its absence," or the "artistic community as a dissensual one," or aesthetic efficiency as "paradoxical [in that it] is produced by the very break of any determined link between cause and effect."[11] What is useful to remember, amid this amiable climate of suspension of judgment, is that the meaning of a term depends on context even here, so a paradox cannot be the pairing of terms that would form oxymora irrespective of context. The contradiction emanates from the very pairing itself. For example, a sari and a cell phone have no intrinsic contradictions to offer until they're paired as "tradition versus modernity" or "east versus west" in the service of a journalistic agenda. Why would "dissensual community" be any different?

You can often sense when the curator, artist, or critic is pursuing ambivalence and ambiguity in the name of political circumspection and aesthetic incommensurability and when it's a matter of laziness or careerism. But more often than not, the lines are not clear. Goldsmiths scholar Andrea Phillips has recently been conducting research on the figure of the "prop." A prop is neither present nor absent, neither a full-on narrative device nor a mere decorative object. As such, it's a useful figure through which to symbolize and summarize what Phillips terms the "weak politicality" of the field of international contemporary art.[12] Which is where paradoxa create an atmosphere of successful global communication in the room, of networked forms of living and working, and thereby promise some vaguely democratic potential. But allow me to end this essay by pointing out that there's little sense in calling for a great post-ambivalent yonder when the overall political atmosphere outside the field offers little more than the weak politicalities within.

1. James Elkins, *What Happened to Art Criticism?* (Chicago: Prickly Paradigm Press, 2003).
2. Irit Rogoff, "What is a Theorist?" in *Was Ist ein Kuenstler?* eds. Katharyna Sykora et al. (Munich: Wilhelm Fink Verlag, 2004). See http://www.kein.org/node/62.
3. Terry Eagleton, *The Function of Criticism* (London: Verso, 1984), chapter 5.
4. Hito Steyerl, *Die Farbe der Wahrheit* (Vienna: Turia +

Kant, 2008), 139–40.

5. Harold Bloom, *A Map of Misreading* (New York: Oxford University Press, 1975), 102.

6. Paul de Man, "Criticism and Crisis," in *The Blindness of Insight* (London: Routledge, 1983), 3.

7. Elizabeth Diller, "Bad Press," in *The Architect Reconstructing Her Practice*, ed. Francesca Hughes (Cambridge, Mass.: The MIT Press, 1998), 76.

8. Eagleton, *The Function of Criticism*, chapter 6, 114.

9. Boris Groys, "Critical Reflections," *Art Power* (Cambridge, Mass.: The MIT Press, 2008), 111.

10. Thomas Demand, Mark Godfrey, Jörg Heiser, Jennifer Higgie, Adrian Searle, et al. "Binary Fluffing," *frieze* no. 100 (summer 2006), 220–25.

11. Jacques Rancière, "Aesthetic Separation, Aesthetic Community: Scenes from the Aesthetic Regime of Art," *Art and Research* 2, no. 1 (summer 2008).

12. Andrea Phillips, "Objects, Props, Assemblages," in *Showroom Annual: Props, Events, Encounters* (London: The Showroom, 2008), 2.

Tom Morton

Three or Four
Types of Intimacy

In his essay "Homage to the Half-Truth" (1991), the late British art critic Stuart Morgan writes that "chief among myths that underlie the critic's task might be that of Cupid and Psyche"[1]—a tale of a woman joined in darkness each night by an anonymous male lover who forbids her to light a lamp lest she discover who he is. Curiosity, though, gets the better of Psyche, who one night illuminates their bedchamber, the better to stare upon Cupid's sleeping form. In the moment she recognizes him for the god he is, she mistakenly pricks herself on one of his arrows, deepening her ardor and provoking her to kiss him, an act that causes her to overturn the lamp, splashing his bare chest with hot wax. Waking with a start, Cupid calls an immediate end to the affair. Total identification has brought about a total and irreversible rift between the lovers, and no mortal or immortal hand can wrestle the cat back into the bag.

Morgan, however, has a different take on the myth, claiming that its basis is not "identification at all, but recognition akin to that which a critic feels: some sudden awareness of a pattern that was previously only intuited, a flash of similarity between what is inside and what is out, between self and other, or of mental and physical distances brought about by the experience of loving, or at least of attraction."[2] What is important for Morgan is not the pinning of the butterfly to the board, but the wheeling, net-in-hand pursuit of it over the meadow. What is important is not judgment ("to be judgmental," he writes, "is only finally the case"[3]), but the intimacy that precedes it.

Criticism is, it seems to me, an endeavour that turns on a set of intimacies: between the writer and the work, the writer and the artist, the writer and the reader, and the writer and him- or herself. To write even a short piece of criticism (a review, say, of some hundreds of words) is to spend a considerable stretch of time thinking about a body of work. When was the last occasion, I wonder, that any of us honestly sat for hours or days in silence contemplating nothing but our beloved? For Boris Groys, at least, it seems that in the early years of our young century, this is time squandered. In a recent interview with critic Brian Dillon, the Russian thinker claimed that contemporary art criticism is significant only in so far as *the critic creates a search engine for the reader; fundamentally, he just says "Look at this!" Whatever is said beyond this is perceived merely as an explanation or legitimization of this advice to look. People are not so interested in why they should look at it; they're interested in whether they should look at it at all. They're also not interested in the critic's opinion....*[4] Consequently, says Groys, as a critic, *you have to decide what you want to advertise, what your ideological position is, what you want to make known. Of course, you're no longer interested in criticizing anything; you're interested in forwarding what you think is interesting for you, what should be regarded as interesting for culture in which you are living, what you're ready to support.*[5] Even worse, *being a writer, the art critic does what a writer generally does: he talks about himself. Under the pretext of explaining his position he begins to write.... And if the critic is a good writer, we read him as we read any other writer; just as a text, just as writing.*[6]

Groys is, to a degree, being playful here. As Dillon asserts in an earlier review of Groys's volume of essays *Art Power*, he is *surely right to suggest (albeit ironically) that the much-rumoured decline of critical authority is in fact an unprecedented opportunity.... Radical, even Utopian, impulses are hidden today in seemingly enfeebled institutions and practices.*[7] That having been said, it is perhaps worth treating the markers of decline identified by Groys with a dose of skepticism. There are certainly those who subscribe to the notion that any publicity is good publicity, and there are certainly artists whose careers have been buoyed by great stacks of press clippings, favourable or not, although this cannot be said to be the sole secret of their success. (Do, say, museums really program exhibitions and acquire works on the basis of what Groys calls the "digital code" of contemporary criticism: "zero or one, mentioned or not mentioned"[8]?) Equally, there are readers who, from time to time, use certain types of criticism, most often newspaper criticism, as more of a "what's on" guide than anything else. I am not sure, though, that we read criticism "just as text, just as writing," or even that I know what this apparent demotion means—a novel, a paper in a scientific journal, and the copy on a cereal box are, after all "just text, just writing," but each of them has a markedly different purpose and appeals to markedly different types of authority. The critic may, as Groys says, "talk about himself," but it's hard to think how this might be avoided—we have nothing but our better or worse selves through which to process the world. There is, after all, no possibility of a super critic, producing super text or super writing. Discontented as some of us may be with human frailty, we cannot transform the shambling journalist Clark Kent into Superman.

At the age of twenty-two, a few months after I had concluded my formal education, I wandered, without knowing it, into a profession in crisis. Call it "art criticism" or call it "art writing," this field of activity had, according to numerous commentators, apparently become if not untenable, then at least deeply problematic. Some blamed, as Raphael Rubenstein wrote in his 2003 essay in *Art in America* "A Quiet Crisis," a combination of the post-structuralist aversion to hierarchies with a generalized Valley girl-like vapidity that created an intellectual environment in which, in Rubenstein's memorable phrase, "value judgments and the quest for historical significance are so yesterday."[9] Others, such as Suzanne Perling Hudson, blamed the art market, which, as she claimed in her 2002 essay for *October*, "Beauty and the Status of Contemporary Criticism," now requires from the critic nothing more than "beautiful writing about beautiful objects and their beautiful makers."[10] Still others blamed the ascendancy of the curator—a position exemplified by Maria Lind's assertion in *Manifesta Journal* that "most of the interesting discussions over the last ten years have been formulated in projects, from collaborations between artists, curators and other people—on the floor of an institution, but not through writing."[11]

Today, ten years after I first wrote about art in exchange for money, these apparent pressures on criticism have, if anything, only increased. Commercial gallerists exert more influence on the way artists' work is framed than perhaps ever before, currently the curator seems to have the upper hand over the critic in the arm wrestling match over who gets to be the prime mediator of contemporary art, and there remains a useful and, for some, frustrating uncertainty about, if not ascribing value, then about dubious notions such as "genius," "masterpiece," and "canon." Does this add up, then, to a crisis in criticism? I'm not so sure. The art world I was born into is not, it is certain, a Panglossian best of all possible art worlds (life within it can be, in Hobbes' formulation in *The Leviathan*, 1660, "nasty, brutish and short"), but neither is it somewhere in which the critic is a mere copywriter, or a madman ranting, alone and ignored on the trackside, as the great goods train of the market, or the nomadic caravan of curatorial practice, rumbles blithely past. If the critic is willing to ask where is freedom and adventure, and what does it mean to be awake, there remain messy, plural answers to be found.

frieze, the magazine at which I began my critical career and for which I still work, has, in Britain at least, been the focus of much of the formal and informal debate surrounding the so-called crisis in criticism. Typically, the accusations leveled at the magazine include a tendency towards "belletrist" writing, an emphasis on the affirmative over the negative, and, rather less seriously, that it possesses an "in-crowd" mentality (don't all magazines have that?), and, my personal favourite, the charge that *frieze* is "sooo *frieze*." The belletrist accusation is especially instructive, containing as it does the claim that proper criticism must be couched in the texture-free language of an operating manual or academic treatise, and anything else must be the meretricious stuff of, as Hudson put it, "beautiful writing about beautiful objects and their beautiful makers." This, though, is to confuse plainness with plain speaking, lyricism with lying, and the avatars of these critical approaches with Roundheads and Cavaliers. Language, even the language of the operating manual, is never neutral, and the appearance of objectivity is, in the end, precisely and only that. Perhaps what is really being played out in these accusations of "belletrism" is an anxiety about the critic somehow trespassing onto the artist's territory and dipping an inappropriate toe into the waters of creativity. To create, though, is not necessarily to deceive. If the novelist may tell a truth about the particularity or universalism of human experience without recourse to the language of the academy, surely a critic may tell one about that much smaller thing, a work of art? There is, then, it seems to me, no such thing as "appropriate" critical language, save perhaps that which a particular work elicits from the writer, tempered by their wider understanding of the world and all that it contains. Elsewhere in her *October* essay, Hudson wrote that what she calls "beautiful writing" now "fills the spaces left vacant in the evacuation of strident critical activity."[12] It's hard to think of this as much more than tribal politics. To get down and dirty with art, to feel its grain and let it feel yours, is subjective, sure, but it is also the most meaningful critical activity I can imagine. To refuse this is to refuse the fact that all of us cast a shadow and that it will sometimes fall across a work of art, not only obscuring it but also, and perhaps paradoxically, making it in a strange way whole. Only vampires, after all, possess no shadow, and a vampire is something a critic should never aspire to be.

Back, for a moment, to the charge that much contemporary art criticism is relentlessly affirmative, one that might be repudiated by an examination of that seemingly most humble of critical activities: the exhibition review. The leading art magazines *(Artforum, frieze, Flashart)* carry anything between ten and forty reviews, often published in a separate section at the magazine's rear end. While some titles carry lead reviews of over 1,000 words, the average review clocks in at somewhere between 500 and 750 words. In almost every case, no biographical information is given about the author of these texts, whatever their status in the outside world. On these particular pages their words are presented with equal weight. Reviews sections often function as an unofficial audition space for new critical voices. Non-writers might be forgiven for thinking this is a soft landing—surely 750 words are easier to wring out than a lengthy lead feature, and surely a single exhibition provides an imitable structure, a frame for one's critique, that the diffuse stuff of an artistic practice does not? I'm not so certain. Delivering a successful review demands much of a writer, not least that he or she interrogate what the criteria of "success" might be. As auditions go (and even established critics are always auditioning, always stepping nervously onto the stage), it's a tough prospect. You dance your dance in public wearing homemade ballet shoes. No second take. No erase and rewind.

While it might seem obvious, it's worth pointing out that the review occupies a particular place in the spectrum of art writing. While the monographic magazine feature or catalogue essay may be assumed, with the odd exception, to be broadly affirmative (few journals expend large numbers of pages on art that they do not in some sense support, and still fewer commercial or public galleries knowingly publish texts that undermine their business interests or institutional authority), this is not necessarily true of the review. Here the gloves, or at least all bets, are off. No reader, and certainly no interested party, should be able to tell how a given show has been received by merely scanning the contents pages of a magazine. Reviews sections, then, at their best offer up something rare and rather precious—a space in which art and curatorial practice may be assessed that's insulated against the noisome buzz of power, money, and prior reputation, if not against the critic's own flawed self.

If the review is about writerly freedom, it's also about responsibility, not least to a magazine's readership, to many of whom the reviewer is a necessary proxy, an ocular stunt double employed to see shows they'll never see themselves. Most writers who have visited an exhibition with the purpose of reviewing it will have felt the flickering presence of the future reader at their elbow, chiding them not only to look and think harder, but to do so with an eye and mind that are not quite their own. This is more difficult than the dubious notion of critical objectivity assumes. While it's clear that the reviewer cannot approach a show as *a* viewer in the casual, go-on-impress-me sense (criticism isn't about whether a work of art rubs you the right way), neither can he or she approach it as *the* viewer—that mythical composite of you, me, and everyone we do and do not know. Caught up in the wobbly magnetic field generated by these two poles, they must develop a mode of address that is true to their subject matter, their readership, and themselves—one that evokes the absent exhibition rather than merely describes it, and one that evaluates it in terms broader than those provided by personal preference or any one *prêt-a-porter* theoretical position. If anything still signals critical authority (and if we can still usefully employ that term), it may be the ability to do this.

To write a review—to write anything—is to compromise, and the first compromise is always forced by time. The frequency with which most art magazines are published means that the reviewer has only a few weeks to shuffle thoughts into words—a fresh insight or shift in perspective might arrive, unbidden, after their copy has been filed, but this is not a business that deals in "Director's Cuts." Space, too, in the form of a word limit, has an effect: while it's comparatively easy to parse every work in a small solo show, reviewing a large group show or biennial means presenting, at best, a partial account, and so a partial truth. Other (self)-limiting factors are more in the reviewer's control—a knowledge gap can be plugged, a prejudice can be examined and lanced (or disclosed)—but the most wakeful of them are always aware of the beautiful, maddening failure of their project, which is to say the failure of language in the face of anything but itself. And yet, if every review ever written is furred by time, space, and the clumsiness of words, this is not something that is peculiar to the form. As with all writing, what matters here is honesty, along with the hope that one might communicate against the odds.

Exhibitions, unlike most art works, are transitory things, which eke out a second life through catalogue essays and documentary photography. What this material cannot capture, however, is how a show has worked on those uninvolved in a particular time and place. Given this, perhaps the most important function of exhibition reviews is to make solid the ephemeral stuff of reception, to write a history of attention, both to art and to the way it snags on the world and on the self.

Turning again towards the notional "crisis in criticism," it is worth focussing for a moment on the economics of the profession. Anyone who writes about art knows that it is not well paid, and very few freelancers can get by on this type of work alone. One consequence of this is that in those sections of the art world that are in thrall to money, the critic is often considered to be a marginal, somewhat scruffy, and curiously old-fashioned figure. Another is that many critics are not only or even primarily critics, but also work in other fields, including, significantly, curating. To some degree, the idea of being both a critic and a curator might seem paradoxical—surely one cannot be a poacher and a gamekeeper at the same time? This is to forget, however, that historically art criticism has rarely been the sole activity of those who best practice it (think, for example, of Giorgio Vasari, Charles Baudelaire, John Ruskin, or Robert Smithson) and to set up what Alex Farquharson described in a 2005 essay as a "mock antipathy" between criticism and curating that "conceals the convergence of the two."[13] As Farquharson states: *Most curators write criticism at one time or another, particularly when not working for an institution. It is hardly surprising, then, that some of these former curator-critics have helped make the institutions they now work for more discursive by emphasizing publishing and discussion. Although critics may not dominate the discourse in the way they once did, there's little doubt we still need an independent forum within which the ideas of artists—and curators—can be analysed and evaluated. Otherwise, art's archive will consist entirely of producers' accounts of their own activities—and we've all seen how misleading and self-serving these can be.*[14]

Farquharson's point is, I think, important, and it underlines the fact that while art criticism seems unimportant, or at least infinitely manageable, to commercial art world interests, it is its intellectual marginalization by elements of the curatorial sector that, if anything, will plunge it into crisis. If a class of independent, prominent, and well-remunerated critics is not something the current art world feels it can afford or even really wants, those who do practice criticism are more necessary than ever. Theirs is the first draft of art history, written in the heat and intimacy of a first encounter. It is also—and herein lies its highest value—a historical deposit itself.

1. Stuart Morgan, "Homage to a Half-Truth" (1991), in *What the Butler Saw*, ed. Ian Hunt (London: Durian, 1996), 234.
2. Ibid.
3. Ibid.
4. Boris Groys in conversation with Brian Dillon, "Who do you think you're talking to?" *frieze* no. 121 (March 2009), 126–31.
5. Ibid.
6. Ibid.
7. Brian Dillon, "Art Power (book review)," *frieze* no. 117 (September 2008), 43.
8. Boris Groys in conversation with Brian Dillon, "Who do you think you're talking to?" 126–31.
9. Raphael Rubenstein, "A Quiet Crisis: Is there a serious breakdown in the dialogue around contemporary painting?

Should art critics get back into the business of making value judgements?" *Art in America* (March 2003), 41.

10. Suzanne Perling Hudson, "Beauty and the status of contemporary criticism," *October* no. 104 (spring 2003), 115–30.

11. Alex Farquharson, "Is the Pen Still Mightier?" *frieze* no. 92 (June–August 2005), 118–19.

12. Suzanne Perling Hudson, 117–18.

13. Alex Farquharson, 118–19.

14. Ibid.

Sven Lütticken

A Tale of Two Criticisms

Modern art criticism is twice born, having been shaped by the mutual influence of two opposed yet interwoven critical traditions. One lineage is that of Enlightenment criticism, instigated when a certain Étienne La Font de Saint-Yenne arrogated himself the right to judge the French Salon in the name of the Public with his 1747 pamphlet *Réflexions sur quelques causes de l'état present de la peinture en France*.[1] The other is that of Romantic criticism, for which we do not have quite such a clear and convenient beginning. What Romantic criticism is, or could be, is scattered across the early writings of Friedrich Schlegel, Novalis, and others in their circle, around 1800.

The different natures of these beginnings, their differing degrees of publicness, are themselves significant. In La Font's time, the idea of a general public for which, and in whose name, one writes was still new and subversive. To claim that one had the right to judge the productions of French painters was an attack on the absolutist state and its king (an academy patron); to find the art sponsored by him severely wanting was also to suggest, however implicitly, that the system that produced such art was lacking. Soon, Johann Joachim Winckelmann would draw complex analogies between the nature of Greek art and the political freedom enjoyed by the classical Athenians; such reasoning was by no means uncommon. Small wonder that Denis Diderot, who would become the most important Enlightenment critic of art, published his Salon reviews not in print, but in the hand-copied *Correspondance littéraire*, which was sent to select subscribers or "correspondents."

Enlightenment criticism passed judgments in the name of a public that it had to posit, or forge, in the first place, and such judgment had a moral dimension that was not always implicit: Diderot attacked François Boucher as a man whose conception of art could be only lowly, his imagination having been dragged down by the cheap prostitutes in whose company he spent his time.[2] Romantic criticism radically reconceptualized the work of art. Far from having to obey "eternal" rules posited by the critic in the name of the public—rules that regulate the representation of suitable subjects in a manner that is morally edifying and ennobling—the work of art is now seen as establishing its own shaky rules, which the critic tries to reconstruct. In Jacques Rancière's words, the era of early Romanticism marks the moment when the work of art comes to be seen as an "object of thought"—not merely in the passive sense, but as an object that is itself a manifestation of mute thinking, of intuitive theory. Positing an incommensurable rationale of its own accord, the work of art confronts the viewer with a tangled knot of reason and its other, of *logos* with *mythos*.[3] This means that the relationship between the critic and the work is stood on its head: struggling to do justice to the work of art, which, if successful, is a law onto itself, the Romantic critic himself becomes the object of an implicit judgment by the work of art. Will he (at first, the critic was, of course, almost always a "he") do justice to its inner workings, or fail the test and have recourse to irrelevant criteria? While the risk of failure is thus a very real one, the Romantic critic also aims higher than his Enlightenment counterpart: at its most ambitious, Romantic criticism not only sought to do justice to the work of art's inner workings, but also to raise its idiosyncratic logic to a plane of greater self-awareness.

In his famous dissertation on *Der Begriff der Kunstkritik in der deutschen Romantik* (1920), Walter Benjamin argued that the task of art criticism as conceived by the early German Romantics is to elevate the work of art to a higher plane of reflection; Friedrich Schlegel referred to his own essay on Goethe's *Wilhelm Meisters Lehrjahre* as the *Übermeister*.[4] Yet we are not dealing with a linear Hegelian process in which the obtuse manifestations of Spirit in the work of art are liberated from their sensuous shackling by being raised to the sphere of pure reason; instead, we are dealing with an ironic, endless dialectic—an endless series of reflections. This is criticism as critique: *"Criticism," in its Enlightenment sense, consists in recounting to someone what is awry with their situation, from an external, perhaps "transcendental" vantage-point. "Critique" is that form of discourse which seeks to inhabit the experience of the subject from the inside, in order to elicit those 'valid' features of that experience which point beyond the subject's present condition.*[5]

A crucial example of the Romantic criticism of visual art is Clemens Brentano and Achim von Arnim's 1810 text on Caspar David Friedrich's *Monk by the Sea*, *Verschiedene Empfindungen vor einer Seelandschaft von Friedrich, worauf ein Kapuziner*, which takes the theatrical form of a series of written sketches of scenes in which visitors to an exhibition comment on the work in ways that, above all, emphasize their education and worldly preoccupations—and say preciously little about the work, except for the myriad of different approaches it seems to generate and to frustrate.[6] When Heinrich von Kleist radically reworked the text's introduction for his newspaper *Berliner Abendblätter*, he wrote that looking at the painting, with its unprecedented emptiness and *Uferlosigkeit* (unboundedness), made him feel like his eyelids had been cut off.[7] While this might suggests the possibility that the painting is at fault—that the artist has pushed things too far, beyond the bounds of what can be called art—it is telling that Kleist, like Brentano and von Arnim, resisted the temptation to jump to conclusions.

After all, a painting's apparent deficiencies may be un-known qualities, and the critic needs to be on his guard.

* * * *

These two opposing concepts and practices (for in each case we are dealing with a concept that is put into prac-tice, or a practice that generates a concept) have largely dominated art criticism for more than two centuries. This is not to deny many crucial changes that have taken place. In fact, understanding modern art criticism in terms of a dialectic of Enlightenment and Romantic criticism can benefit the analysis of such transformations—and enable us to see some aspects of the contemporary situation with greater clarity.

One crucial transformation of Romantic criticism was its historicization and politicization. Romantic criticism was always latently historical; after all, modern art is a problematical object of thought precisely because it has lost its self-evident, conventional status. However, in the later 1920s, Benjamin concluded that Romantic critique had given way to a reductivist and ahistorical form of "im-manent" criticism, and in order to counter this he proposed a Marxist notion of strategic criticism. This dialectical criticism shares with the immanent approach "the refusal to judge work according to given criteria," since "there is no position from outside the work from which the critic may judge it," as Howard Caygill put it. *The critic must find the moments of externality within the work—those moments where it exceeds itself, where it abuts on experience—and to use them as the basis for discriminative judgment. Strategic critique moves between the work and its own externality, situating the work in the context of experience, and being in its turn situated by it.*[8] Radicalizing Romantic criticism, this kind of dialectical critique sees the work of art as incomplete insofar as it can never fully resolve the historical contradictions it articulates more or less successfully.

It is worth recalling that Clement Greenberg's art criticism emerged in the context of the Marxist critical project that was the *Partisan Review* of the late 1930s. However, in Greenberg's case the project of thinking through art's contradictions under industrial capitalism soon morphed into something else—into the justification of one kind of modern art as superior. In concluding his 1940s essay "Towards a Newer Laocoon," Greenberg stated: *I find that I have offered no other explanation for the present superiority of abstract art than its historical justification. So what I have written has turned out to be an historical apology for abstract art. To argue from any other basis would require more space than is at my disposal, and would involve an entrance into the politics of taste—to use Venturi's phrase—from which there is no exit—on paper. My own experience of art has forced me to accept most of the standards of taste from which abstract art has derived, but I do not maintain that they are the only valid ones through eternity. They are simply the most valid ones at this given moment.*[9]

The tensions running through this dense passage would never be resolved by Greenberg; if anything, the circularity of his reasoning became ever more pronounced. On the one hand, he deferred to History—to a reductivist, closed version of the historical dialectic. On the other hand, his specific value judgments were increasingly justified with summary references to his superior eye, his experience; supposedly the outcome of the same historical process that created the art he judged, Greenberg's personal taste was thus supposedly attuned to history and to art, and in that sense immanent. However, in the course of the 1960s, as Greenberg increasingly rejected much of the more interesting new art, he came

to look more and more like an old Enlightenment critic, passing judgment in the name of laws that had little to do with
the art. In the early 1960s, Greenberg's historical model had
appealed to young critics, many of whom wrote for *Artforum*, but by the end of the decade the more ambitious of
these critics saw the limitations of Greenbergian formalism
quite clearly. Rosalind Krauss documented this process in a
number of texts, including "A View of Modernism," in the
September 1972 issue of *Artforum*.

Greenberg was frustrated by development that art criticism took in 1970s and 1980s; he faulted critics for replacing the question "Is it good?" with the more neutral one of
"What does it mean?"[10] Of course, Greenberg had extremely
limited definitions of both "quality" and "meaning"; whereas for Greenberg these are different, the younger critics followed Benjamin in practicing a form of criticism that sought
to judge not *ex cathedra*, but by thinking through a work's
inner logic in its historical context, and if necessary beyond
its limitations. The journal *October*, founded in 1976, was the
most important medium for this project; its title signaled a
return to an avant-garde model that had first been obscured
by Greenbergian Modernism and that faced further threats
from the market-driven pluralism that emerged in the 1970s,
leading critics such as Rosalind Krauss to abandon *Artforum*
in favor of a project dedicated to a new version of "strategic
criticism"—one dedicated to Benjaminian "discriminative
judgments" rather than Greenberg-style pronouncements
on "great art" and "minor art."

* * * *

October's historiographical and theoretical achieve-
ments can hardly be overstated, but how successful was
this project as strategic, dialectical criticism? After all, such

criticism does not conceive of itself as existing in a vacuum; it is part of the historical process. In the case of *October*, the journal's revolutionary (Eisensteinian) title sits in an odd contrast with its status as an academic journal. If strategic criticism survived in *October*, it is perhaps largely as a potentiality rather than as an actuality.

Meanwhile, most art magazines publish a debased version of Romantic critique. The Romantic "completion" of the work of art is turned into a theoretical virtuoso performance that above all seems to aim at strengthening the author's position on the market. The specialist criticism published in magazines and catalogues functions as market-driven romanticism that uses infinite reflection to avoid arriving at some sort of judgment; it finds its counterpart in the increasingly beleaguered reviews in newspapers and other mass media, which often amount to a debased Enlightenment criticism that offers judgments without reflection. When art magazines publish top tens and "best of" lists, it would appear that what matters is less what is being said, and more that something (of whatever nature) is being said about a certain artist or show—by a certain critic or curator. And is the same not true of newspapers? While the space allotted to reviews has been decreasing over the past ten to fifteen years, papers have increasingly taken to "translating" the content of a review into three or four out of five stars and publishing lists of "shows worth seeing." In the latter case in particular, judgment has been reduced to the mere act of mentioning.[11]

One might conclude, as Boris Groys has done, that "yes/no" or "plus/minus" judgments are anachronistic and ineffective.[12] The only form of judgment that still functions, Groys argues, is "one/zero" criticism; the judgment lies in the decision to write about an artist or show, or not. In a way, this has been the modus operandi of Romantic criticism all along; after all, all only a good work of art demands and deserves textual "completion." But one/zero criticism is hardly the triumph of Romanticism; if anything, it signifies the entropic collapse of both historical models. In Romantic criticism, the one/zero form of critical judgment was largely a side effect; what really mattered was to engage with those works that seemed to demand it. Now, however, the one/zero judgment has moved from the margin to the center, in the process transforming not only Romantic criticism but also Enlightenment criticism: critics may still pass yes/no judgments, but these could now be seen as surface phenomena that distract attention from the real judgment. The "no" of every negative review is negated by the fact that the review was published at all—by the fact that it is a "one."[13]

To observe the features of the current textual landscape is a beginning, but it is not enough. That all forces seem to be aligned in favour of this form of criticism does not mean, as Groys seems to suggest, that there is no room for interventions in this critical regime. A fundamental problem of the current form of one/zero criticism is that its judgments remain implicit and thereby unquestionable. Surely discourse would be impoverished if none of us were prepared to criticize an artist or project outright and put our own criteria to the test—to risk opening ourselves up to the criticism that we have not been attentive enough to an artwork's complex logic, that we might have failed dismally to produce an *Übermeister.* However, I would argue that to continue the inherent and implicit work of reflection in a critical text is also to be attuned to the work's contradictions and aporias, which may be more or less serious and detrimental to this work's success. To practice "completionist" criticism, then, does not preclude value judgments, but these will be rather different from those of Enlightenment criticism with its apparently fixed criteria. Especially in its historicized and politicized form, as Benjaminian strategic criticism, the practice of Romantic critique does indeed arrive at judgments—but these spring from taking the work of art's logic (faulty as it may be) to a point where it goes beyond and against the work's limitations, where it is confronted with other logics operating in its cultural and historical context.

Following Andrea Fraser's suggestion that art criticism should be practiced as a site-specific activity, it seems to me that part of the job for a critic writing for art-world publications that tend to neutralize debate (magazines, catalogues) is to try to push reflection to the point of site specificity.[14] This can also mean writing about artists one has serious doubts about—even if it may contribute to their status and increase their symbolic capital. This is a price that has to be paid for breaking the deafening silence. If writing in art magazines and catalogues needs to push reflection to the point where its interpretations become discriminative judgments, other forms of criticism need more reflection on the *a prioris* and aporias of evaluating art. It is probably too late in the day to worry about traditional newspaper criticism; more relevant is the Web, in particular, blogs. Here, site-specific criticism would mean capitalizing on the informality of the Web in a way that goes beyond proud displays of personal preferences. Media that are not traditional platforms for criticism of visual art can also be fruitful, and in establishing connections between different media, site-specific criticism may become truly strategic. Turning against the limitations of the media in question, such criticism may momentarily open up spaces for partisan reflection amidst the ones and zeros.

1. On La Font, see Thomas Crow, *Painters and Public Life in Eighteenth-Century Paris* (New Haven and London: Yale University Press, 1985), 7–11.

2. "Et que peut avoir dans l'imagination un homme qui passé sa vie avec les prostituées du plus bas étage?" Denis Diderot, "Salon de 1765," *Salons,* vol. II (Oxford: Oxford University Press, 1960), 75.

3. See, for example, Jacques Rancière, *Le Partage du sensible: Esthétique et politique* (Paris: La Fabrique, 1998), 30–40.

4. Walter Benjamin, "Der Begriff der Kunstkritik in der deutschen Romantik" (1919/1920), in Rolf Tiedemann and Hermann Schweppenhäuser, eds., *Gesammelte Schriften I.1: Abhandlungen* (Frankfurt am Main: Suhrkamp, 1991), 67.

5. Terry Eagleton, *Ideology: An Introduction* (London and New York: Verso, 1991), xiv. The distinction between criticism and critique is specific to the English language; German, for instance, knows only *kritik*.

6. See the published version, with Heinrich von Kleist's editorial changes, "Verschiedene Empfindungen vor einer Seelandschaft von Friedrich, worauf ein Kapuziner" (1810), at http://wendelberger.com/downloads/Kleist_Seelandschaft.pdf.

7. Ibid., 4.

8. Howard Caygill, *Walter Benjamin: The Colour of Experience* (London: Routledge, 1998), 62–63. Benjamin's "Programm der literarischen Kritik" (1929–30) is in Rolf Tiedemann and Hermann Schweppenhäuser, eds., *Gesammelte Schriften VI: Fragmente, autobiografische Schriften* (Frankfurt am Main: Suhrkamp, 1991), 161–67. I am indebted to Esther Lieslie for pointing me towards this text.

9. Clement Greenberg, "Towards a Newer Laocoon" (1940), in John O'Brian, ed., *The Collected Essays and Criticism 1: Perceptions and Judgments, 1939–1940* (Chicago and London: University of Chicago Press, 1986), 37.

10. Alice Goldfarb Marquis, *Art Czar: The Rise and Fall of Clement Greenberg* (Boston: MFA Publications, 2006), 237.

11. This development has been pronounced in the case of the so-called "quality newspapers" in the Netherlands and much less so in, for instance, Germany.

12. Groys recalls that, when he was writing for a newspaper, he *very quickly understood that people reacted only to the fact that I had written a text, that this text was published in the newspaper, had a certain length, was illustrated or not, and was or was not run on the front page of the feuilleton section. They absolutely didn't react to what I wrote, be it description or evaluation, and they absolutely couldn't distinguish between positive and negative evaluation…. I understood immediately that the code of contemporary criticism is not plus or minus; I would say it's a digital code: zero or one, mentioned or not mentioned. And that presupposes a completely different strategy, and a different politics.* "Who Do You Think You're Talking to? Boris Groys in Conversation with Brian Dillon," *frieze* no. 121 (March 2009), 126–31.

13. Confusion over this issue abounds. Recently, an artist whose work I had dared to criticize in print sent an irate letter to the editor of the magazine in question, complaining that my remarks would undermine the market for his work in the US. I highly doubt that any negative judgment in the text would outweigh the effect, such as it is, of writing and publishing the text in the first place.

14. Benjamin Buchloh, Hal Foster, Andrea Fraser, David Joselit, Rosalind Krauss, et al, "Round Table: The Present Conditions of Art Criticism," *October* no. 100 (spring 2002), 223.

William Wood

Notes on the Demise
and Persistence of Judgment

Some commentators have located the demise of judgment within the massive proliferation of art styles in the closing decades of the twentieth century. Others have laid the blame at the feet of such culprits as the recently inflated art market and the legacy of institutional critique.[1]

I want to discuss the framework for the *Judgment and Contemporary Art Criticism* forum as spelled out in the organizers' printed *Supplement* and through texts selected and reprinted there.[2] Through these texts, I would like to bring in historical and contemporary references to the conditions leading to our old friend, the putative, recurring crisis in art criticism. With that crisis in mind, and before addressing the impact of proliferating art styles, the inflated art market, and the legacy of institutional critique, I want to touch on a quote which has strong implications for the matter of judgment and art.

Art, considered in its highest vocation is and remains, for us, a thing of the past. Thereby it has lost for us genuine truth and life, and has rather been transferred to our ideas instead of maintaining its earlier necessity in reality and occupying its higher place. What is now aroused in us by works of art is not just immediate enjoyment, but our judgment also, since we subject to our intellectual consideration (i) the content of art, and (ii) the work of art's means of presentation, and the appropriateness or inappropriateness of both to one another.[3]

The quote is from Georg Wilhelm Friedrich Hegel's *Lectures on Aesthetics*, last delivered in 1828. I raise Hegel's reconsideration of art because, on the one hand, we can say that it engages a massive Wincklemann-like fantasy:

the fantasy of citizens of ancient Athens walking familiarly among polychrome statues, or the equally erroneous vision of the Gothic cathedral as decorated with the "bibles of the illiterate," both of which represent ideals of past art emphasized in forms of Romanticism contemporary to Hegel. Yet, in this fantasy, I want to note how Hegel's emphasis on art's belatedness encourages us to underline separation from art in our consideration of it. Meanwhile, the equally powerful desire to overcome that sense of being separate persists, whether in the revered spontaneity of Abstract Expressionist brushwork or the immediacy stressed in some accounts of conceptual art or behind a more current investment in the simulacra of community achieved through social practice or "relational aesthetics." The pain of separation and distance, encapsulated in the notion of art being "a thing of the past," which decisively divorces the present of forlorn art from its integrated past, is at least partially (maybe substantively) compensated for by endorsing and exalting judgment. As Hegel has it, art provides "not just immediate enjoyment" but calls us to judge appropriateness as well. Acknowledging that dreams of reconnection persist alongside the compensating reassurance of judgment, I wonder whether both constitute linked foundational fantasies: that is, fantasies of reconnection persist because we want always to imagine not being alienated from art, while, simultaneously, judgment—although promising finality—insists that we are, at least intellectually, constantly at a distance from art.

I came to Hegel's reconsideration of art through the end-of-art thesis propounded by critic and philosopher Arthur Danto. In his *After the End of Art*, the idea that the proliferation of art styles in the closing decades of the twentieth century has impact on judgment can be fairly easily associated with his discussion of what he calls a democracy of pluralism in contemporary art. Danto claims that "there is now no special way a work of art must be," tracing this condition back to Andy Warhol's *Brillo Box* of 1964, which possesses no significant distinguishing visual difference from the Brillo box found in the supermarket.[4] While Danto has much more to say about that example, his point is that Warhol's box signals the end of that notion of the "special way art must be," which he attributes to what he calls the Age of Manifestoes. Broadly coincident with the period of post-Hegelian modern art and culminating in the rise of the avant garde and the neo-avant garde, the Age of Manifestoes is marked by practices of inclusion and exclusion which dictate that certain types of art work exemplify the most significant art and that all other contemporary art is inferior, perhaps not art at all. This declaration of inclusion and exclusion is an exceptional type of judgment where discrimination takes first place. One of the most often discussed example of this sort of exclusive judgment is Michael Fried's 1967 "Art and Objecthood" (discussed mainly by Fried himself in subsequent writing). There, modernist painting and sculpture as distinct media and the theatricality of minimal art are opposed in a manner whereby, combining aesthetic with theological judgment, Fried could emphatically declare that "theatre and theatricality are at war today, not just with modernist painting…but with art as such."[5] Such exclusive judgment is presumably what critic and curator Christopher Bedford wants when he calls for a return to Clement Greenberg-style "critical criteria," a "well-organized, well-argued, and clearly explicated system of value."[6] Yet Fried's essay is remembered and expressly recalled as a bellicose swansong for a type of critical *diktat* which purported to offer exclusive judgment while actually being special pleading based on "an attack on certain artists (and critics) and a defence of others."[7] Bedford may point favourably to the richness of the debates that ensued, but I have doubts that anyone today could find in medium specificity sufficient grounds, or fervent faith in certain artists as righteous proof, truly to emulate Fried's 1960s example—except Fried himself in his 2008 monographic paean disguised as an explanation of *Why Photography Matters as Art as Never Before.*[8]

In her essay "Change and Criticism: Consistency and Small Minds," also from 1967, Lucy Lippard is already preparing ground for moving away from the excluding mode when she argues that "a judgment on contemporary art is *tentatively* true, like a scientist's law and unlike a legal law."[9] This comparison of types of laws indicates something which Fried's call for medium specificity cannot tolerate, for she is encouraging looking not to a canon but to experimentation for criteria in engaging art and criticism. When Lippard goes on to say that "the critic's role is descriptive rather than prescriptive," combined with her allusion to the scientist, she points towards the oft-forgotten attraction of technocratic adventures such as communications and systems theory and the philosophy of science—as elaborated in books such as Thomas Kuhn's 1962 book *The Structure of Scientific Revolutions*—on contemporary thinking about the arts and culture in the 1960s. Besides indicating an expanded field beyond media specificity, one outcome of this attraction which Lippard seems to be anticipating was her own subsequent practice as a descriptive critic of the conceptual art that overtly tried to avoid or render useless the categories of painting and sculpture—not to mention aesthetic conviction and cultural privilege—which upheld the exclusionary judgment of critics like Fried, as well as her later inclusive approach to feminist and activist art projects and her concern with aspects of locale in her writing.

We can see the legacy of this move from prescriptive judgment to tentative description operating in the *October* round table when David Joselit speaks of judging "what constitutes an object…an object of history and object of aesthetic interpretation"[10] or speaks of judging "the boundaries of a field"[11] in the context of engaging both art and visual culture. Joselit is making a double move. On the one hand, we need to judge what is an appropriate object for criticism, as when a critic passes over the phantom of the "thing in itself" to determine how the work of art is articulated and refracted through institutional framing, curatorial context, and the histories, conventions, and subjects it emerges through and calls upon. On the other, where do the bounds of aesthetic interpretation lie? Are art critics (or art historians who act as critics sometimes, like Joselit) and their competencies able to reach meaningfully to other areas? Are we (since I occupy the same field) in possession of specially pertinent tools and analyses which might be fruitfully applied to a broader range of images and objects, from popular culture, non-elite spectacle, and subcultural practices? I do not want to get caught up in this question, but want to argue that this double move means that we need to come closer to considering not the proliferation of styles but the proliferation of *objects* and the proliferation of *aspects* in the field of contemporary art and criticism. For Sven Lütticken, the issue pivots on the distinction Joseph Kosuth is credited with elaborating between "specific" and "generic" art, with generic or art-in-general being a situation where "objects nowadays exhibited as art no longer derive their legitimacy from a tradition or an artistic medium but from the very fact that their artistic status is initially dubious."[12] Such a proliferation of objects for contemporary art has a consequence that, to Lütticken, differently politicizes the sort of pluralism Danto cheers on as democratic. Since art can include most anything, it is then open in a new way to the commodity relations of spectacular society, and so the artist has become an exemplary consumer. Meanwhile, the sort of criticism which stresses art's "potential for dissent and difference" risks being merely the "marketing slogans for art that has sabotaged such a project," promoting its consumption in a deceptive, probably repressive, but incrementally different type of pitch.

In response to this potential sabotage, Lütticken (with a nod to Boris Groys), discusses Marcel Broodthaers, seeing him as a figure whose acts of consumption amounted to "not merely a reflection *of* spectacle but a reflection on it" and further claims that this sort of "meta-consumption" can result in "decoding, deviant commodities which are more thought-provoking and productive compounds" of the "irrational rationality of the spectacle."[13] Though he appears to laud this tendency—and to link it to other scripto-visual artists like Dan Graham and Robert Smithson—Lütticken is also concerned with the way in which the "ideology of art" stipulates that the culture industry represents the big Bad Cop while the art business represents the Good Cop— the one who "is good for people, refined, complex—and critical." Aware that critical writing—whether or not it is exclusively judgmental—is part and parcel of art's privileged position as something somehow regarded as not entirely instrumentalized, Lütticken writes of the uninflected importation of contemporary cultural theory into artistic and critical discourse as often constituting unreflective consumption, what he calls a "pathetic, pathological tangle of slogans and hype."[14] Here we might also consider Julian Stallabrass's contention that a good deal of contemporary art's charm lies in the way it acts as a cipher for notions of artistic and creative freedom while simultaneously being nicely positioned as spectacle in the status stakes played out by powers who are bent on increased capital accumulation through increasing inequity.[15]

We are now up against the question of the recently inflated market and its impact on judgment. Is this really a problem? Many commentators on contemporary criticism, including Lütticken and James Elkins, write of an imperative that art must appear with some form of writing attached to it and, equally that there has recently been more publishing of commentary, gossip, blogging, publicity, and art writing than ever before. In addition, Elkins claims that most of what is produced is not read and certainly not worthy of close reading.[16] Meanwhile, in a 2008 discussion of "Art and Its Markets," Tim Griffin, editor of *Artforum,* said that the abundance of advertising in his magazine had lead him away from the market to areas where he could use the ad revenue "to do something completely counterintuitive: slow down, be late, even slightly out of sync."[17] Hence, the magazine had recently featured articles and tributes to figures seemingly extraneous to the fungibles of art dealing and collecting—philosopher Jacques Rancière, dancer Michael Clark, novelist Alain Robbe-Grillet among them. In this example, the judgment of "an object of history"— which Joselit upheld—sustains what Hal Foster calls "the archaeological function" of criticism,[18] returning the forgotten or revaluing the marginal thanks to revenue from a market whose interests it, nominally, does not represent— though here, we must recall that reviving marginal figures extends the stock available for dealing.[19] As well, dealing, whether in words or of works, can come to have reciprocal effects by generating subsequent circulation of works and in words.

I am not, like Dave Hickey, an apologist for the art market, but diffidence about the art market's relationship to questions of criticism and judgment necessitates neither an embrace of the ubiquity of market pressures nor a disavowal of those pressures. Rather, we can look to the art market's many contradictory aspects—the lack of a clear sense of what art is worth, what it can do, how it is promoted simultaneously as token of freedom and as owned object, as luxury goods and as cultural patrimony, as things useless as instruments but viable for all sorts of speculative purposes.[20] These questions are grounded in matters of autonomy and heteronomy, the two poles which, according to Pierre Bourdieu, structure the field of cultural production, making its nineteenth-century French formation "the economic world reversed."[21] (To revise the terms for the field of contemporary art in the recent past, we might speak of the art market as representing the economic world synchronized.) It is not that the market dictates criticism—Tim Griffin wondered: "Could a publication seriously damage *anything* anymore?"[22]—but to recognize that inflation in a bubble market and especially the corrosive effects of presuming market relations to be the prevailing model for social life has taken on the character of a neoliberal monolith, resulting in the eradication of remaining vestiges of publicness while endorsing weak citizenship.

In front of the Richard Serra-like monolith, we might turn away from the art market towards the question of funding and governance of public institutions like museums. As Andrea Fraser points out in the 2002 *October* round table on "The Present Conditions of Art Criticism," the privatization and corporatization of museums and galleries is the result of "a historical shift" since the 1970s where: "The progressive ambition of building audiences for art museums…[whereby] museums began to recognize that they had publics and public responsibilities, as did artists and critics and curators" came to be "seen through the prism of professional and institutional needs."[23] As she concludes: "So art for art's sake was replaced by growth for art's sake—which was often seems a thin cover for growth for growth's sake." This is somewhat related to an argument brought forth by Benjamin Buchloh concerning how one "target" of conceptual art's thorough criticism of the field of contemporary art in the 1960s and 1970s was "the secondary discursive text that attached itself to artistic practice." As he further states, "readers' competence and spectatorial competence had reached a level where the meddling of the critic was historically defied and denounced."[24] What interests me here is the trend to revise the relatively recent past regarding the encouragement of "democratization and decentralization"—in the progressive bureaucratic language of the day—in postwar cultural organizations and individual reception. That is, to see how laudable aims that pointed away, again, from exclusive judgment and inherited privilege, need to be understood as plays in a field where every part is active and unforeseen consequences need to be exposed and subject to analysis. If, in the museum, opening up the institution to more publically sensitive accountability also advanced administrators' adoption of corporate methods and standards, so the redirected energies of the empowered viewer/reader of conceptual art could also be seen to contribute to the quelling of the exclusionist critic as well as a harbinger of intensified heteronymous, inclusive forms of art writing—like gossip, blogging, and publicity. A further implication is that, just as the corporate methods of the museum stress attendance numbers and fundraising goals, so inclusive modes of art writing remove barriers to publication along with the residual conscientiousness of the professional critic.

This brings me to the legacy of institutional critique inasmuch as Buchloh is credited with its initial analysis and Fraser is surely one of its most articulate practitioners. Indeed, Fraser offers perhaps one usable definition of criticism: "I define criticism as an ethical practice of

self-reflective evaluation of the ways in which we participate in the reproduction of relations of domination, which
include for me the exploitation of competence and other
forms of institutional authority."[25] It is through "self-reflective evaluation" that institutional critique causes problems
for judgment since critique and reflective thought demand
questioning of the authority of those who present themselves fit to judge. Taking this definition into consideration
leads Fraser to recommend a "site-specific" type of art
criticism that means "not misrecognising your readership
as the other of your discourse but as the actual people who
are probably going to be picking up the magazine and looking through its pages."[26] Sven Lütticken comes to a similar
conclusion when he writes of the possibility that the "ideology of art" which sponsors Good Cop/Bad Cop notions
can also permit "fragile alliances between institutions and
individuals in the art world."[27] This, to me, is a large part of
the legacy of institutional critique because Lütticken and
Fraser not only recognize the importance of critique and
contextualization but they also display an abiding involvement in the institutions they subject to critique. Such investment has always marked the strongest manifestations
of the critique of institutions—the ethically sound conviction that Hans Haacke held that his 1971 real time social
system, *Shapolsky et al. Manhattan Real Estate Holdings,*
would be shown at the Guggenheim Museum because of-
ficials would recognize its public importance. In the end,
of course, they did not: Director Thomas Messer enacted
and excited subsequent critique by cancelling the exhibition, proving the limits of tolerance within the notionally
liberal establishment. In this example, the legacy of institutional critique prompts judgment of matters of exclusion
and inclusion in cultural life and questions those "relations
of domination" we all participate in by venturing that the

description or re-description of institutional conditions leads towards attempts to fulfill repressed and latent potentials otherwise not considered.

Having discussed the three factors leads me to propose some tentative conclusions:

1. If we move from regarding the proliferation of styles to considering the proliferation of objects or the proliferation of aspects in the field of contemporary art, we realize that the actual difference is that we no longer judge works but assess or analyze projects or practices. Partly this is an effect of a shift in the way artists produce work; artists no longer make works but prepare exhibitions—they make shows. Again, although one can trace this back to the decline of state and private commissions and the ascendance of the commercial gallery in the late-nineteenth century, the most obvious example is the "post-studio" condition of the 1960s when artists like Carl Andre or Dan Flavin had component parts delivered to the gallery and assembled the show there. One might go further and, recalling that a Flavin requires a certificate to distinguish it from directly store-bought fluorescent fixtures, agree with Boris Groys when he argues that much of what we approach as contemporary art in galleries and museums is not art work but art documentation that depends on art being "no longer present and immediately visible but rather absent and hidden."[28] This means that we may personally *prefer* certain examples but we can no longer faithfully argue that this video is better than that photograph on secure, pseudo-connoisseurial grounds.

2. The recently inflated market is an aspect, maybe an extremely volatile aspect, of the relations of domination whereby art and culture are part of the "dominated dominant" portion of social life. The feints and moves of all the agents in the field affect judgment not by dominating it

in the literal sense of dictation, but by inciting all manner of play between autonomous and heteronomous positions and dispositions. This is not meant to be comforting but it does offer, though critique and analysis, the possibility of plotting the players and comprehending their moves in relation to each other. Once we cease judging by appeal to an impossible autonomy and recognize the inevitability of heteronomy, we see that it takes ingenuity rather than faith to manoeuvre in the field.

3. The legacy of institutional critique is best understood as an unrelenting ethical imperative, as Fraser put it, speaking of her own practice, "to perform the inseparability of freedom and determination; to perform that contradiction without distancing it in facile irony or collapsing it in cynicism."[29] With talk of freedom and determination, we can return back to the quote from Hegel and note something latent in his writing which might be more explicit in my description of the replacement of exclusive judgment with the judgment of objects of interpretation and of aspects of the field of contemporary art. Namely, that art is not now in pursuit of its highest vocation but the memory of that vocation and the idealism it entails persists in rumours and fantasies that art has become alive again under new circumstances. Though the idea is tantalizing in many ways, I hope we can also see that it is tremendously unlikely to be so.

1. *Supplement for Judgment and Contemporary Art Criticism* (Vancouver: Artspeak and Fillip, 2009), 5. This booklet included reprints of texts by Lucy Lippard, Sven Lütticken, Christopher Bedford, and James Elkins, as well as "Round Table: The Present Conditions of Art Criticism," *October* no. 100 (spring 2002).

2. The *Judgment and Contemporary Art Criticism* forum was accompanied by a reading room/gallery installation and a brochure publication, both put together by Fillip and Artspeak. Besides mapping the overlapping territory that prompted the collaboration leading to the forum, these coordinated opportunities to read the texts and handle the products of criticism also offered the speakers and the audience selected writings and provided the hint of a history to consider prior to and following the two days of papers and discussion. For a list of texts included in the *Supplement*, see Bibliography, page 169.

3. G. W. F. Hegel, *Hegel's Aesthetics: Lectures on Fine Art*, trans. T. M. Knox (Oxford: Clarendon, 1975), 11.

4. Arthur C. Danto, "Three Decades After the End of Art," *After the End of Art: Contemporary Art and the Pale of History* (Princeton: Princeton University Press, 1997), 35.

5. Michael Fried, "Art and Objecthood," *Artforum* 5, no. 10 (summer 1967), 12–23, as reprinted in *Art and Objecthood: Essays and Reviews* (Chicago: University of Chicago Press, 1998), 163.

6. Christopher Bedford, "Art Without Criticism," *X-tra* 10, no. 2 (winter 2008). I could add that one can say that Greenberg had a "clearly explicated system of value" only if you forget about the various and often conflicting attempts to sort out his position by critics and historians such as T. J. Clark, Thierry de Duve, Charles Harrison, Caroline Jones, Rosalind Krauss, and Barbara Reise.

7. Fried, "Art and Objecthood," 167.

8. Michael Fried, *Why Photography Matters as Art as Never Before* (New Haven: Yale University Press, 2008).

9. Lucy Lippard, "Change and Criticism: Consistency and Small Minds," in *Changing: Essays in Art Criticism* (New York: E. P. Dutton, 1971), 24.

10. Benjamin Buchloh, Hal Foster, Andrea Fraser, David Joselit, Rosalind Krauss, et al, "Round Table: The Present Conditions of Art Criticism," *October* no. 100 (spring 2002), 209.

11. Ibid., 217.

12. Sven Lütticken, *Secret Publicity: Essays on Contemporary Culture* (Rotterdam: NAi Publishers, 2006), 8.

13. Ibid., 14–15.

14. Ibid., 14.

15. Julian Stallabrass, *Art Incorporated: The Story of Contemporary Art* (Oxford: Oxford University Press, 2004).

16. James Elkins and Michael Newman, eds., *The State of Art Criticism* (New York: Routledge, 2008), 72–74.

17. "Art and Its Markets: A Roundtable Discussion," *Artforum* 46, no. 8 (April 2008), 300.

18. "Round Table: The Present Conditions of Art Criticism," 220.

19. Along with the "Art and Its Markets" roundtable, the April 2008 issue of *Artforum* has a discussion of how a sizeable posthumous market for the work of Lee Lozano has been generated through a "circle of belief" consisting of fellow artists, critics, curators, dealers, and collectors. See Katy Siegel, "Market Index: Lee Lozano," *Artforum* 46, no. 8 (April 2008), 330, 390.

20. For a study of at least one aspect of this complex and contradictory diffidence, the pricing of works of contemporary art, see Olav Velthius, *Talking Prices* (Princeton: Princeton University Press, 2005).

21. Pierre Bourdieu, "The Field of Cultural Production, or: The Economic Field Reversed," *The Field of Cultural*

Production, ed. Randal Johnson (New York: Columbia University Press, 1993), 29–73, 273–79.

22. "Art and Its Markets," 300.

23. "Round Table: The Present Conditions of Art Criticism," 213.

24. Ibid., 205.

25. Ibid., 214.

26. Ibid., 223.

27. Lütticken, 16.

28. Boris Groys, "Art in the Age of Biopolitics: From Artwork to Art Documentation," *Art Power* (Cambridge, Mass.: The MIT Press, 2008), 53. On the subject of Flavin's certificates, see James Meyer, "The Minimalist Unconscious," *October* no. 130 (fall 2009), 143–76.

29. Andrea Fraser, "Performance Anxiety," *Artforum* 14, no. 6 (February 2003), 103.

Maria Fusco

Say Who I Am[1]
Or a Broad Private Wink[2]

I had two books with me, which I'd meant to read on the plane. One was Words for the Wind, by Theodore Roethke…. My other book was Erika Ostrovsky's Céline and His Vision. Céline was a brave French soldier in the First World War— until his skull was cracked. After that he couldn't sleep, and there were noises in his head. He became a doctor, and he treated poor people in the daytime, and he wrote grotesque novels all night. No art is possible without a dance with death, he wrote.3

Re-imagining the art object as sharing a number of basic ontological qualities with the riddle, I am interested in thinking through some ways to write about, or, again, write around the art object: to elicit, to unlock, to *induce* its essential obscurity with essential obscurity.

Approaching the writing of this text, I looked back at my original précis and discovered that I had used a very wrong word. In fact, the use of this wrong word was a fundamental error on my part, and thankfully, now that I've realized this, I can proceed with the proper word (or so I hope).

My wrong word was *deduce*.

In summoning this word, I had inadvertently evoked the very fixed place where I had hoped not to be; for to deduce, with the dictionary smack of reaching a conclusion or inferring something from a general principle, is far from my understanding contemporary art writing. What I'm interested in is what art writing *might* be, rather than what it actually is.[4]

What I really should have said was *induce*.

For to loiter near the art object, with the intention of capture through critique, should essentially be a procedure of *induction* rather than of *deduction*, in that we are creating or tracing a broader, possibly more fertile environment through close looking, rather than tracking a logical conclusion from the clues given. To concur with Maurice Blanchot, as he would have it in his 1941 novel *Thomas the Obscure*, "making no distinction between the figure and that which is, or believes itself to be, its centre, whenever the complete figure itself expresses no more than the search for an imagined centre."[5] It's preferable, then, to work in the margins, to attempt to write "the inside meaning of it if you understand me."[6]

We should keep in mind, after all, that the supposed ur-deducer Sherlock Holmes had but detailed knowledge of "everything" that could be applied to his inductive investigations of crime, but little to no knowledge of the material world outside of his investigations.[7]

I would suggest then that this intensive focus is inductive in nature, for its methodology is essentially open-ended. Sherlock Holmes's investigation isn't over until it is over, but he is not a typical detective. For those detectives who start from an *a priori* point of certainty, an assumption of who perpetrated the crime, progress along a static path of discovery is based on this "fact," which leads them to reach the conclusion that they had already came to in the first place. On the other hand, Holmes's approach is not one of surety. He doesn't come to the crime knowing who has done it; rather, he induces it.

We can see Sherlock Holmes's inductive approach (the approach of the conscientious critic, perhaps?) in Arthur Conan Doyle's first Holmes novel, *A Study in Scarlet* (1887), in a comment made by Holmes to Watson: *Most people, if you describe a train of events to them, will tell you what the result would be. They can put those events together in their minds, and argue from them that something will come to pass. There are few people, however, who, if told them a result, would be able to evolve from their own inner consciousness what the steps were which led up to that result. This power is what I mean when I talk of reasoning backward.*[8]

This backwards reasoning demonstrates that Holmes has not made his mind up but proceeds with alertness and tact. And again, this backwards reasoning is temporal in nature—traversing past-production that is no longer accessible (the artwork), shot through a present of inscription (the examination), towards a future that will probably be barely dented by our observations (the marketplace); without this reasoning, however, there cannot be a full understanding of *what* or *why* (the role of the art critic).[9]

Critical art writing that harbours at its core an aggregate problematizes (yet also harmonizes) its subject; to borrow an observation of Marie Darrieussecq's, "The unsaid is that which advances literature, that which it explores as a virgin or submerged land. Ghosts are born of the unsaid.… To write is to give a voice to ghosts."[10] How best to explicate this "unsaid" without resorting to a mere process of critical translation, object to text? Why, to read and write the object simultaneously: more precisely, to write as you read.

All of this, of course has direct implications not only for the validity of the judgment procedures of art criticism, but also for its direction, speed, and methods of approach.

Let's reconsider Sherlock Holmes's impulse to reason backward in relation to an observation from Michel Tournier in his autobiography *The Wind Spirit*, an observation in which we may catch strains of the faint scent of critical methodology: *…in all good philosophy the solution always precedes the problem. The problem is nothing but the shadow cast by its solution, a fountain of clarity that spurts motu proprio into the empyrean of the intelligible.*[11] Whilst I would not necessary hold with, or even particularly desire the type of clarity that is generally assumed to be of use to culturally assemble (or is that re-assemble?) a "complete" art object—rendering it less leaky, and therefore more substantive or even marketable from any viewable angle—I would like to spend some more time re-imagining how backwards movement might help us to "assess" the art object more clearly, that is, to further the purposes of parlous (here meaning difficult or uncertain, rather than its homophone *power*less) navigation.[12]

But then there's backwards movement, and there's backwards movement.[13]

A fundamental principle of Cartesian analysis suggests that when given a problem to be solved, we examine the conditions to be fulfilled, dividing them into simpler conditions that are themselves easier to solve, to go backwards, so to speak, from the given problem to the simpler and solvable constituents. *This* type of backwards movement presents a problem, however, in art writing, in terms of how to divide, sort, or again order the parts into a form that seems easier to inspect. The "ordering" action, by its very nature, suggests a sequential or narrative thrust toward a specific destination, the place of judgment—not, I would suggest, a very useful movement in criticism, and one that is often characterized by descriptive rather than inscriptive processes.

The kind of backwards movement that interests us here is more closely identified with the seemingly counter-intuitive dynamism of Maurice Blanchot's "Orphic Gaze": its power to inspect, to vaporize, to transform. Blanchot has said in his essay "The Gaze of Orpheus": *At first sight, the image does not resemble a cadaver, but it could be that the strangeness of a cadaver is also the strangeness of the image. . . . What is left behind is precisely this cadaver, which is not of the world either—even though it is here—which is rather behind the world . . . and which now affirms, on the basis of this, the possibility of a world—behind, a return to backwards.*[14]

This "return to backwards" depicts a resistance, or perhaps more exactly, a sly challenge to comprehension, highlighting as it does the essential obscurity of the image—or here, as we are terming it, the art object—thereby suggesting that it must be approached in a different way, and, just as the cadaver itself is in a state of "infinite erosion," so too is the art object, in terms of its physical presence, together with its cultural and economic currencies.[15] Contemporary art criticism nurtured by the appearance of value may be both witness to—and witnessed to be—assembling an inauthentic absolute object or teratological corpus through rationalist grafting of interpretation from scrappy parts: criticism demanding to be read of itself, whilst simultaneously calling for a re-reading of something that is outside of itself.

We can look to less orthodox modes of criticism to examine the dissolution or dissemination of the absolute object in the same way as we look to fiction to lead us on an aporetic procedure, enacting critical judgments through question after question rather than answer after answer.

Criticism *can* cajole objects to speak,[16] but we must be prepared to accept that these very same objects may only be able answer us in riddles. Furthermore, we must be prepared to approach art objects in a riddlic form, in order to elicit the most sophisticated or productive responses. Non-traditional, more experimental methods of critical art writing can help. This complex object, this art object, may, by speaking, shed itself of the soup stowage of deductive judgment value, encouraging us to develop the catoptric approach of being reader and writer at the same time: or again to *write* as we *read* the object critically.[17]

Monsieur Teste, Paul Valéry's eponymous antihero, asserted that "God made everything out of nothing, but the nothing shows through."[18] Perhaps it is the very "nothing" of the art object that may be interrogated and indeed celebrated as half-intended discovery through the backward reasoning of more experimental modes of critical art writing, but only if that very same writing is willing to embrace, and, yes, even to embody the inherent obscurity, the delicacy, the dispersive excursion of induction.

1. Daniel Tiffany, "Lyric Substance: On Riddles, Materialism and Poetic Obscurity," *Critical Inquiry* 28, no. 1 (2001), 73.

2. Flann O'Brien, *The Third Policeman* (London: Flamingo, 1993), 117.

3. Kurt Vonnegut, *Slaughterhouse Five* (St. Albans: Panther, 1972), 21.

4. Two flights up to the gallery, Linda was greeted at the door by the gallerist John. His eyes looked very puffy, like he'd been crying for a long time, or eaten something that hadn't quite agreed with him. Linda caught the track of a thin acrid whiff emanating from John's threadbare overcoat; a coat that looked like it might once have been navy blue, but was now simply there.

5. Maurice Blanchot, *Thomas the Obscure* (New York: David Lewis, 1973), 3.

6. O'Brien, *The Third Policeman*, 167.

7. "Now Linda. What do you want? All of it? Do you want to see all of it?" John unhooked a key from beside the door jamb where he was still wedged.

"Yes please John. Everything you've got. I'd like to include a good selection in the piece. I think it's important the readers get a sense of the range of the work."

8. Arthur Conan Doyle, *A Study in Scarlet* (London: Penguin Classics, 2001), 123.

9. "Yes, so vibrant…those colours…" Linda was very impressed by the stark contours in the photographs; their texture and timbre wound up something tight inside her. The body seemed to be lying right on top of the page rather than sitting within it; thickly applied make-up coated the surface of the skin: a glossy rainbow. It was all surface. And what was on the surface was good.

10. Marie Darrieussecq interviewed by Becky Miller and Martha Holmes in December 2001. See http://uri.edu/artsci/ml/durand/darrieussecq/en/eninterview2001.html (accessed January 2, 2009).

11. Michel Tournier, *The Wind Spirit* (London: Methuen, 1991), 125.

12. Linda always shaved the top and the bottom of her legs, as she ran the razor slowly and carefully up the inside of her thigh, the soap scum dropped off the blade in heavy grey clumps, weighed down with stubble in the thin layer of water.

13. Instead of stopping shaving at the top of her thighs, Linda kept on going, and dragged the razor up to where her legs joined her body. She paused. She paused to lather more soap in around her pubic hair. Even though the hair was thick and coarse, the hot water had softened it and the razor was new, so she shaved off the top layers without much difficulty. Linda had to keep rubbing in lots of soap, working in small patches, until all of the hair had migrated into the bath water, where it floated, suspended in spindly scum. She ran her hand over the area and when it all felt smooth, she stopped shaving. Still wet, Linda fetched her little round magnifying mirror from the bathroom cabinet. It struck Linda she had never had a really good look at her own cunt—not properly anyway. Now, with no hair

the little mauve mollusc seemed more shrivelled than it had ever done before. Not too bad though. Not too tattered. But not as nice as the cunt in the photograph.

14. Maurice Blanchot, *The Stationhill Blanchot Reader* (Barrytown: Station Hill Press, 1999), 439.

15. John had laid out a selection of the original spreads out on the table, but this time, he'd arranged them into a narrative sequence; one in which the model crawled across the pages, twisting and stretching her limbs into each corner. The darkness of her cunt penetrated each page like a hole bored by an impatient reader.

16. Linda lay down on the gallery floor whilst John held the first magazine for her to see, so that she could get the position right.

17. When John finally approached her, Linda was surprised not by its size—for that was just as she'd imagined—but by its colour, monochrome, engorged with blood yet its very surface lifeless.

18. Paul Valéry, *Monsieur Teste* (London: Routledge and Kegan Paul, 1973), 101.

Diedrich Diederichsen
Judgment, Objecthood, Temporality

Some time ago, I began playing a game with myself: whenever a gallery opening threatened to be boring, I compared every art object at hand with *The Simpsons* episode that aired the same afternoon. I probably don't need to tell you that, in most cases, the cultural industrial product of three scriptwriters, three hundred Korean draughtsmen and women, several actors, and many other people was not only more intelligent, funny, and entertaining than its counterpart, it also succeeded on the home turf of fine art: a self-reflexive discussion of its own means in order to achieve a specific aesthetic goal: justification of that goal.

This game interrupts high art's dream to live in a perfect world in which human production is not measured and debated on the grounds of normative ideas and criteria. This dreamworld—in which art exists outside of the rules of cultural industrial production—is not pleasant. It is a hellish, petit-bourgeois dystopia in which people play games without winners and the idea that anything is preferable to anything else is grinned away by zombies who avoid conflict by any means.

Judgments, especially negative judgments of value, have increasingly bad press. Opinions are supposed to be relative, debates open, and results postponed. The widespread attitude among artists and curators these days is that recipients (many single people) would rather interact than judge. Theoreticians seem to agree. Complaining about this is similarly widespread. Here, I agree with Tirdad Zolghadr's remark that complaining about the lack of judgment is as widespread as judgments are absent.

But to support the notion of judgment is not necessarily

to call for a return to order, as Zolghadr suggested in his keynote address. It may as well be a leap forward, a re-definition of disagreement on the basis of argument instead of taste; a re-rationalization of distinction against its naturalization. Only the ironicist, who observes discourses not for their argumentative, transitive value, but for their object value (beauty, rarity, newness, complexity)—an almost a hegemonic intellectual type these days—will refuse this possibility. He or she avoids right/wrong alternatives by all possible—and often dandyistic—means. I have certain sympathy for this attitude based on historical merits that date back to the days of a hopelessly deadlocked but still hegemonic critical discourse. But I disagree in the contemporary situation, in which an avoidance of judgment is not only held to be natural, it is also politicized in a semi-heroic rhetoric. These were the programmatic and normatively anti-normative statements of the 2006 Viennese conference *Kritik* on the state of the art of criticism: *What is critique? It is certainly not simply a practice of judging, much less of condemning. It may be that these kinds of reactive, abbreviated forms of "critique" charged with resentment are still being preached from the pulpits of academic teaching and announced from within the bunkers of art criticism, a practice that is perhaps even stronger than ever. In a contemporary concept of critique, however, it can no longer be a matter of a more or less rigorous yes or no to a certain object.*[1]

I would indeed agree that it is reductivist to limit critique or criticism exclusively to judgment; one could say, for example, that this would identify the process with the result. But certain things in these programmatic sentences irritated me: "Condemning" and "negative judgment" are "stronger than ever"? Where? In which "bunkers of art criticism," and where in the discourse of "academic teaching"? Where are you living? If there is one thing you never read anywhere nowadays, it is a negative judgment against any show, project, book, or catalogue by anyone involved in the fine art world—this simply does not exist any more. The reason is that, in all likeliness, producing negative criticism results in social death. Writers would need the support of other structures, outside of the art market, to achieve the social power to negate any object or project within it. But, on the other hand, to adequately address contemporary art, one needs so much insider knowledge that criticism from outside is hardly possible and not even desirable.

There is a similar situation in newspaper journalism and in many specialist discourses such as film criticism. The only exceptions, at least in the European situation, are the-atre and classical music. Here, at least in some old-school bourgeois newspapers—which nobody takes seriously anyway—the editors keep up a traditional form of review culture in which negation is still possible. This often leads to a widespread misunderstanding: judgmental criticism is possible only within traditional fields. In today's complex contemporary art world, you can only guess the value of art in general. But if traditional rules don't apply within con-temporary art criticism, the social rules that make certain art beautiful for specific people are based on judgments and their defence. Every conversation about contemporary art progresses through disagreements, exposure of criteria, and so on. The unexplained absence of these discursive habits in written art criticism fulfils even the easiest criteria for some kind of false consciousness or ideology —that is what a certain discourse hides and that it is hiding it.

I want to support a practice of criticism that eventually produces judgments—of course not final, holy judgments, but judgments of value. Eventually, I hope to come up with some ideas for a certain practice of judging that I will find defendable, as opposed to the pseudo-noble withdrawal from judgment. But first I want to discuss an antagonistic constellation that I found in one of the texts of another Viennese symposium on critique and criticism, organized by the same European Institute for Progressive Cultural Policies that was responsible for *Kritik* in 2006. In his introductory lecture for the conference *The Art of Critique* (2008), Gerald Raunig refers to distinctions based on Foucault's text "What is Critique?" and a reading of Foucault by Judith Butler.[2] In this discussion, Raunig makes a distinction between critique as an open process—a general perspective towards the world—and a narrow-minded notion of critique as a practical and useful instrument that helps you get through the world—or rather, helps you decide between consumer options.[3] Raunig quotes Butler as having argued that critique in the first sense is the very process that suspends judgment.

By the way: I found my fellow panellists at the *Judgment and Contemporary Art Criticism* forum well dressed. I like Jeff's jacket, I like Maria's jacket, I like my jacket.

This idea of critique as a process-oriented attitude gravitates towards the description of people, their personal mindset, their self-image, their morality. In other words, it develops a tendency which drives the practice of this process-oriented critique-as-way-of-life towards focussing on issues of the self, a self which is not completely free of petit-bourgeois notions of the value of a self. It does not prescribe the discursive side of a discursive practice, but the personal, psychological, habitual side of it. This critique might still be a discourse, a discursive practice, but in order to conceive of it in that way—as a suspension of judgment—it must be thought of as a discursive activity involving living people, not just critical or theoretical production. This suspension of judgment can make sense only as a quasi-aesthetic and/or ethical practice that organizes itself around the life of thought, its infinity and physicality. It is by no means the asymmetrical activity of people vis-à-vis objects or vis-à-vis the world, which one might associate with critical practice in the first place. Instead it describes people vis-à-vis themselves, how they grow, develop, avoid, play and maybe even produce—but all from a position of sovereignty, self-control, and even narcissism. Maybe this is a deeper reason for the strategies of avoidance and fluffiness that Zolghadr mentioned in his opening lecture. You shy away from judgment because you feel that, in this post-Fordist world, objects, especially art objects, are people or are very close to people. That means that when you judge, you insult someone, not just on a professional level, but on a personal level. We are all far too well educated to do that.

Here is a very different idea of critique or criticism, involving value judgments: I am talking about value judgment and criticism in the discourses of "emergent people"—young, recently immigrated or arrived, recently allowed to speak, and so on—vis-à-vis an already finished world of objects. This position can be found amongst non-emergent populations as well. In Gerald Raunig's introduction, he makes reference to Raymond Williams, via Butler, who argues that one should think of critique as open-ended practice instead of a teleological activity leading to judgments. But it is exactly the possibility of arriving at judgments that makes this particular critical activity an unstoppable one, because it articulates seemingly final decisions all the time. It has to continue forever; it has to permanently rediscuss what it has seemingly been decided for good. Only because a sentence has the seriousness of a final decision and an eternal damnation will it be discussed over and over again.

Of course the subtext of Foucault's, Williams's, and Butler's privileging of a critical attitude, a critical project, over critical judgment is the ethics of politicization, the ethics of political activity or even activism, be it in a revolutionary sense referring to some normative idea of turning your life around, turning it into a responsible revolutionary one, or in a democratic sense, as a normative idea of participation and involvedness, permanent questioning of and constant skepticism toward official truths. It owes its idea of a criticality that reaches the entire body of the critical subject to ideas and lifestyles of the 1960s and after, which are based on the idea that everyone should change their life and live holistically, dedicated to their own ideas, and not by an old, bourgeois double standard. I have to say, anticipating slightly arguments I want to come back to later, that while I grew up in solidarity with these ideas and still hold them dear, I feel I must note at this point that the investment of your whole life, the ethics of a holistic existence, the exploitation not of labour but of life force, is exactly the motor contemporary forms of capitalism are driven by.

Now, in order to go back, this existentialism of the critical position—a slightly polemic exaggeration that is a bit unfair to Foucault, who knew about the dangers of existentialism—is opposed to the seemingly apolitical consumer whose judgments of value are nothing more than judgments of exchange value, or, at best, judgments of a certain economic rationality in relation to a form of use value. They are not free judgments—that is, judgments made outside a relationship to a necessity based on the realities of life.

Aesthetic judgment, in its classical form, at least in the German tradition, is connected to an idea of judgment without relation to a worldly interest in the art object, any use value of it as a thing in daily life. Instead, it is based on a suspension of use and exchange values in favour of a general openness towards pleasure not related to instrumentality and calculable gain. The conditions for the ability or capacity to receive and enjoy artistic objects that particular way can of course be located historically and sociologically; they can be found in a fully developed Western bourgeois culture, beginning somewhere around 1750. They were first studied and systematized by Immanuel Kant in the work that in the English-speaking world is known as the *Critique of Judgment* (1790), although its correct translation should rather be the *Critique of the Capacity of Judgment.*[4] This capacity assumes, without declaring it explicitly, of course, that whomever makes an artistic experience is carefree and socially safe enough to look at an object without desperately needing its use value. You can only enjoy the *peinture* of a still life when the food that it depicts does not make you hungry. This is what Kant calls disinterested pleasure. Bourdieu adds that, of course, only when you're not hungry are you able to remain disinterested.

Identifying this tradition of disinterested pleasure as an element of Western bourgeois culture might be a judgment too, even a condemning one, but I introduce "Western bourgeois" here at first as a technical term. There are two ways to criticize this concept. One follows Bourdieu: to be disinterested is affordable only by the ruling class. Hence whatever this experience might intrinsically be, it cannot be human or universal, since it is constituted through exclusivity. The other critique of this concept does not condemn the concept itself but the uneven distribution of its availability. Maybe there is nothing intrinsically wrong with good wine or pleasant country architecture—only its exclusivity. (This would be a rather Marxist reading of Western bourgeois aesthetic privilege; one would deny a moralist Protestant understanding of privilege.) Maybe the same is true for the disinterested pleasure at the heart of the bourgeois conception of aesthetic experience.

This disinterested affection—at least with Kant—leads

to a specific form of judgment that lies at the centre of social formations. Your highly subjective and untranslatable
experience with an artwork or some other aesthetic object
needs to be communicated. You want to talk about it—and
you have to, in order to socialize in the bourgeois sense,
based on free will, not on necessity. Maybe *disinterested* can
be read as *unforced*, i.e., not driven by necessity, despair, or
need. Positioned as such, aesthetic valuation could be seen
as a perfectly agreeable idea, a kind of utopian break from
the management of daily duties and outside forces (if only
available to some less than others)—a source of socializa-
tion, and maybe the only one we know, that is based not on
your needs but on your unforced subjectivity. Its historical
basis on exclusion is not necessarily intrinsic to the concept, only to its historical formats—which are of course at
least obsolete today if not reactionary.

But whatever our decision about the conception of critique as suspension of judgment, as in Raunig, Butler, and
Foucault, I want to argue that it is also basically an extension of a bourgeois idea of aesthetic experience as essentially unconnected to necessity and instrumentality. But it
is also an extension of the critical impulse from an object
and result-oriented activity to one that includes any human
capacity. Beyond the Kantian idea of a critical judgment as
an individual's attempt to socialize a subjective experience
on the basis of an encounter with an external object, judgment is meant to form an aesthetic basis for how we live.
This would be the aestheticized synthesis of the two previously introduced possibilities of critique as a normative idea
for a way of life and a revolutionary or democratic-partici-
patory break. In an incorporated, fully internalized lifestyle
of critique, even the decision between revolution and reform
is delayed for later since the suspension of object-related
judgments transforms all—including political—decisions

into the eternal postponement of critique as a way of life. The dialectic between extreme subjectivity and the confrontation of the external object tends to evaporate here.

But since this seems to be an ambivalent maneuver, because it is extending the critical impulse, which we agree about, but at the same time limiting it, by cutting off its capacity to interfere by judgment, which we disagree about, I will not pass from my side a final judgment on this discourse. Rather, I will postpone, just as the supporters of this idea tend to endlessly postpone judgment. But I promise not to do so endlessly.

So we have two groups here that I have introduced and two different forms of judging. Group one is judging enthusiastically. They are emergent participants in the market or society in question. They constitute what was once was called "youth culture." But among them you also find social climbers, recent immigrants to a different society, or those recently arrived in a different social stratum. Simon Frith describes their idea of judgment in his book *Performing Rites*: *"Good" and "Bad" or their vernacular versions ("brilliant" and "crap") are the most frequent terms in everyday cultural conversation.... Though all of us knew that what was at issue was personal taste, subjective response, we also believed passionately at times, that we were describing something objectively in the music, if only other people could hear it. Value arguments, in other words aren't simply rituals of "I like/you like." ... They are based in reason evidence, persuasion. Every music fan knows that moment of frustration, when one can only sit the person down and say (or, rather, shout) despairingly, "But just listen to her! Isn't she fantastic!"*[5]

The other group—including Raunig, Butler, Foucault, Williams and the majority of theoretical thinkers in the contemporary art world—shies away from the moment of judgment. They are mostly better-educated academics who do not shout judgments of value at other people. This deep conviction in their education, that a judgment of value is something that you cannot force upon someone else, also shapes their idea of critique as a non-normative, non-conventional endeavour—something that cannot be played by rules because it is precisely about the questioning of rules. And yet if there are no rules, there is also no judgment. This is the program of a critical left that implicitly argues that the lesson from communist and other radical leftist history is the radicalization of a certain unpragmatic relationship towards power and its execution and thus the transformation of its moralistically depoliticized radicalism into an aesthetic position. This last bit remains, of course, implicit and is my polemic.

At this moment you might already smell a conclusion based on a certain class analysis—academic radical refusal vs. young proletarian enthusiasm.

Here, I want to look at the object of these critical positions—if it is really an object at all—and the relation between subjectivity, judgment, and value. The case Frith refers to above developed from a heated debate among music fans on a boat from Stockholm to Britain. In this story, one shouting fan, forcing his enthusiasm upon a non-believer, refers to a song and its singer. Music, although it can be stored and reproduced, altered and rearranged or remixed, has a strange object ontology. It is normally considered to be essentially immaterial and thus not objectifiable. Music fans, of course, have fetishistic relationships to records and other objects related to musical performances, a kind of shared idea of the objectivity and reality of the experience that allows for a meaningful discussion about some record or song. But the experience itself is strongly one of temporality. It is about how things are happening within a time span, which is experienced as beyond the control of the listener or the recipient. You are placed in a time continuum that resembles the way you are situated in the time span that defines your lifetime.

How does one deal with value under these conditions? What is valuable in relation to a lifetime whose length is beyond your control but whose texture is not only not beyond your control but essentially your major obligation? If music happenings occur against time, time is made enjoyable by dividing it up in funky beats, endings are suspended by repetitions, then not, they are played with, all the elements are exposed to a dialectics of convention and surprise—all these occurrences add up to a discussion of the value of life in relation to time: in an anthropological sense as much as in a political sense. This implies that not only openness and contingency, but, more precisely, a ratio between high emotional involvement, and that has to be, to a degree, a passive one and ways out—ways to not become fully subjected to the course of the beats and the chords.

But that is already a description from outside the emotionally involved listening experience, the description of an algorithm of musical enjoyment. Rather, one has to describe the impulse to judge as the main tool, by which listeners position themselves within the continuum that forces them to be emotionally passive. A listener's tendency towards final judgments, total agreement or disagreement, does not only reflect the emotionality of the connection between all time-based-arts to the urgency and the need to decide in real time. This is a characteristic of life itself, especially within a capitalist system where you sell your workforce by the hour. Time based work also appropriates the sovereignty of finality, playing on the temporality of life and its economy. Symbolically this type of work offers the ability to intervene in this temporality to the audience, although they are the ones who are exposed to the temporality in regular life. In a reversal of classic catharsis this is not an effect they experience later, but all the time, whereas the anti-cathartic judgment they use to intervene, to interrupt, to make themselves heard, interrupts the exposure to the domination of time.

Music, in a strict sense—that is, if we don't think of it as a commodity like scores or records—has neither use nor exchange value. It cannot be produced and then later be used like all things that have a use value. It can also not be exchanged for the same reasons. This non-value is, at the same time, its commonality with life itself, which, like music, has a huge value only when connected with a specific human body and specific individual human knowledge. The life of a person, his/her life force, his/her living energy, his/her possible future—all these are not only biopolitical items of investment, but already have represented values for many industries in pre-biopolitical days, when the attributes of liveliness or living energy were still transformed via discipline into old-fashioned labour. But from the perspective of the living being, of the recipient of music, the experience of being overwhelmed lies in the commonality with his/her own life as open and undecided, which causes euphoria or panic. That is why conventions in music are so often needed and welcomed: they anchor it in objectivity and external rules. Judgment helps at least one of its functions, to make the panic and the euphoria tolerable and translatable—to socialize it.

But, at the same time, judgment allows the experience of being overwhelmed to be shared on another, discursive level. Here, the experience becomes manageable, in a cooler temperature, with more distance and sovereignty. It also allows establishing rules around it, building groups and gangs, constructing social scenes and social sense. The judgment of value bridges immediacy and self-organization.

It comes before any other form of reflection. It partly mimics the bureaucracy of regular culture and is one of the most passionate translations of experience into discourse imaginable: this is great/this is crap. It is in this area of tension that the birth of subcultures is situated.

Art objects, on the other hand, have their own management of time. Like music, they are also understood by their recipients in relation to an experience of temporality. But in the case of objects, this temporality is a sublimely endless period of existence. They are either old or incredibly old. They are looked at with the idea of *ars longa*, and that is even a valid idea, if we talk about ephemeral or process- or project-oriented art in the contemporary spectrum. The main idea is that we have time, because the object-related experience is based on the difference between our lifetime (and its sense of temporality) and another temporality not based in human life spans but on truths and experiences that remain to be seen or experienced in the future.

The distinction between art that works only in an immediate relation to our living here and now and art that "has something to say" in a hundred years is normally based on quality or complexity—"old-fashioned" judgments of value. By relating this distinction to the difference between object and process, assigning thus all so-called high art to objects, in a way, and all subcultural art to processes, and then basing these distinctions on the difference between two sensory practices, visual object production versus aural social temporality, we come to another basis for judgments of value that lead to the distinction between art—an investment in the future—and sound—hedonistically taken in, swallowed, gobbled, without any value at all.

Both of these categories of value transcend the Marxist distinction between use value and exchange value. Since both Marxist categories, as I have indicated earlier, rely on the idea that an object or a tool will be used later, can be stored before usage, and can be integrated into some ecology of people and thus build an economy by starting exchange. Music, in its original format, cannot be used later. Art objects can never be properly used, because they exist forever, and forever is always after us. They can be exchanged, yes, but only in an unfinished process of speculation—different from regular speculation, because their exchange value is not based on a specific date.

It is no surprise then, that by constantly judging the first group, emergent people try to symbolically stop the non-reversible passing of their life, whereas the other group, the art historians and political philosophers, avoids judging because this would undermine the very ontology of the art object. But it does not stop there. The aesthetic experience is really endless, but only in relation to the physicality of a mortal human being; the endlessness cannot be experienced in eternity, but in time. In the same way, the total presence of living the experience can only be tolerated by erecting bureaucratic history writing, an attempt to collect experiences like you collect photos in an album. But as much as this activity tends not to develop a reflexive relation to its administration of nostalgia, the relation between speculation, history writing, and the non-objective individual remains non-reflected in many contemporary art debates.

Two historical positions have produced methodologies that might be useful in this context. One is the politicization of pop music, the other is the politicized aestheticism of the Frankfurt School. The various attempts at a politicization—in the broadest sense—of pop music, from Kenneth Anger's *Scorpio Rising* to the Gang of Four, from Red Crayola to Public Enemy, drew from a tension of anti-disciplinary pleasure and the time management of Fordist capitalism articulated in various forms of syncopated or ir-regular rhythmic music and integrated into a larger partici-patory art form based not so much on the expressionism of their protagonist but on their ability to offer territory for projections, debates, and identification—more or less pro-gressive psychological and discursive activities—to the au-dience. There is no doubt that time management became the content of many of the decisive changes in pop mu-sic: massive acceleration (punk) and deceleration (reggae) could mark, at least temporarily, the same change. Gestures and practices of endlessness (improvisation/raves) would also initiate paradigm shifts. In most cases, those were at-tempts to break with the object ontology of music, reap-propriating music as time-based practice. One of its key methods is an uninterrupted practice of judging with the adequate gesture of finality, while at the same time renego-tiating every judgment.

The aesthetic position of the Frankfurt School, on the other hand, as articulated mainly by Theodor W. Adorno himself, but also by some of his followers like the writer, theorist, and composer Hans G. Helms or the musicolo-gist Heinz Klaus Metzger, tried to relocate the work of art and the aesthetic experience with some quasi-heroic ges-ture completely outside of the management of everyday life. Art was positioned outside not only of use degenerated into instrumentality and exchange as the false equivalence of capitalism, but also outside the bourgeois psychological need for life after death provided by art. Thus art's claim was entirely outside the temporalities of bourgeois capital-ism, and at the same time it was its product. It would have to constantly reflexively and negatively deal with these two antagonistic conditions.

Both positions are based on radical assumptions against which one can measure or judge actual results. They produce categories that are not deduced from a pragmatic discourse of art practice but from impossibility and/or negativity. Both positions applaud a euphoric moment that can last only a few seconds, screaming in the first case, or asking for an even more increased negation in the second. Basically, these are the positions that make it possible to realize how a judgment of values relates to temporalities. In the case of the fan of pop music, it's all about the utopia of the moment; for the art or music writer influenced by critical theory, it's all about the critique of bourgeois eternity.

But in both cases, it is history that makes these two types of judgment productive: in the first case, the history of great moments, the history of suspended time, the history of syncopation and suspension of temporality. In the second case, the critique of eternity in the name of history, which might be as long, but as opposed to eternity it is not empty. History not as the narcissistic idea of magnifying life, but of objectifying it: without some necessarily complicated idea of history, judgment is not possible. Especially, the critique of the recuperation of devaluation and revaluation of certain artistic values and values of emancipation by turning them into engines of capitalist production is not possible without the comparatism that looks at the differences between historical stages. You have to be able to think progress in order to criticize regression. Everybody criticizes regression and reactionism, but today nobody acknowledges that any reactionary attack on possibilities of life in our lifetime can be perceived only if your perception is based on an alternative normativity.

1. From the editorial of the symposium *Kritik*, organized by the European Institute for Progressive Cultural Policies, Vienna, 2006. See http://transform.eipcp.net/transversal/0806/editorial/de-en-es.
2. Judith Butler, "What Is Critique? An Essay on Foucault's Virtue," in David Ingram, ed., *The Political: Readings in Continental Philosophy* (London: Basil Blackwell, 2002).
3. Gerald Raunig, "What is Critique? Suspension and Recomposition in Textual and Social Machines," *The Art of Critique*, conference organized by the European Institute for Progressive Cultural Policies, Vienna, 2008. See http://transform.eipcp.net/transversal/0808/raunig/en.
4. Many of the problems with the original (mis)translation of Kant's title have been rectified in Cambridge's 2000 edition of the text. See Paul Guyer, "Editor's Introduction," in Immanuel Kant, *Critique of the Power of Judgment* (Cambridge: Cambridge University Press, 2000), xlvi–xlix.
5. Simon Frith, *Performing Rites: Evaluating Popular Music* (Oxford and New York: Oxford University Press, 1996), 4.

Jeff Derksen
Times and Places of Critique

Today, at the tail end of the long moment of euphoric neoliberalism, the shape of art criticism—and more broadly, cultural critique—is both over-determined and agitated by rapid economic and cultural shifts that have yet to hit their discursive bottom. For, while neoliberalism can be understood in a similar manner to Neil Smith's description of Jürgen Habermas's diagnosis of modernism—"dead but dominant"[1]—it still holds sway as a cultural logic and as a dense force against which all cultural discussion (even if it aims outside of politics) inevitably reverberates. This is simply the historical relationship of any cultural discourse, and any making of culture, to the array of mediations that culture both takes shape within and alters through its own insistence and bursts of imagination. Yet, in the long and troubled relationship of culture to the economic, the embedding of the economic into the cultural (in intensified and perhaps even novel ways characteristic of today) has produced new dynamics.

An affective economy in which value and counter-values are continually measured alongside literal surplus value signals a more profound entangling of art and other creative practices into a world administered through a logic of ownership, a valorization of singularity, a worshipping of surplus value, and a denigration of nonconformist senses of value. While the social revolution of neoliberalism is incomplete, as Habermas said of modernity, it has created a revolution *within* culture by molding the economic into a mediation between all levels of life. In this sense, *the economic* has come to occupy the position of *culture* as the process that holds together the "relationships between elements in a whole way of life," as Raymond Williams famously defined culture in *The Long Revolution*.[2] The economic has also opened itself, in unprecedented ways, to discursive dissection and aesthetic analysis.

Yet these shifts, and the assertion of the economic as the mediating process of the relationships of everyday life, have cohered into a dynamic set of pressures on cultural critique and art criticism that are both globalized and highly localized. This global-local logic, once the defining aspect of culture within globalization, is now central to neoliberalism as a commonsense and migrating form of governance. Locally, the pressures of neoliberal transformation (in the lead up to and wake of the 2010 Olympics) in Vancouver have amalgamated a new set of expectations, contexts, and possibilities for art criticism in the city and beyond. Art criticism and critical discourse is at an extremely potent or even bloated moment in Vancouver. Even in its modest scale, art and criticality have been drawn into a war of values in Vancouver as the city looks to rebrand itself within the nexus of "creative cities" globally. This public transformation is mostly driven by private initiatives, "visions," and power configurations, and it involves the becoming "public" of art at a time characterized by the privatization of public space and goods. Yet the publicness of art is both subtly and heavily mediated through the coherence of civic and urban developers' dreams of the city—a historical configuration of urbanism in Vancouver. The transformation of the texture and "livability" of the city over the last twenty years is intensifying precisely at the moment where the public-private sphere (the public-private partnerships, or 3Ps, which both replace and overlap the public sphere) is becoming more brittle and sterile in terms of democratic processes and more remotely shaped by what Leslie Sklair calls a "transnational capitalist class."[3] In this we can also see a smoothing out of the texture of art and other cultural

production even as enticements (through funding structures) call for art to be more public and to occupy spaces
produced by a complex deal with urban developers that
trades off built and marketable space for public art funding.
In a curious zero-sum game of space (following the myth
that Vancouver has a set amount of space), space for art
is produced as a by-product of another "Vancouverism,"
postmodern residential towers carefully placed so as not to
block the view of our timeless commodity, nature.

Yet, countering the logic of privatization and the reduc-
tion of public art to in-fill building in the urban space trade-
off, in Vancouver we also witness the return of older demands that were to be satisfied by the incomplete project of
modernism: the demand for housing, access to the streets,
more meaningful forms of democracy beyond "stake hold-
ers" consultation, and the call for the return of the imagination in a new urban revolution. It is crucial to ask how art
criticism might imagine itself within this texture of Vancouver—a city with a radical imagination of social protest
and civic organizing *and* a city bursting with boosterism as
its own exportable model of urban success. The complex
politics of the interplay between two of Henri Lefebvre's
categories of space—spaces of representation *and* represen-
tations of space—provides a dynamically critical nexus for
art production and art discourse in this city.

But within this new set of mediations—both global neoliberal urbanism and local rebranding of the city through
culture—gone are the days when we could calmly locate
culture, art, or literature as merely secondary, reflective, or
even outside of the economic. Gone are the days where
we could seek the belatedness, the comfort, or the potential of being merely superstructural, of being miraculously
the last out of the gate and at the tip of the vanguard. But
now is not the time for moping, or tail-dragging, or seeking

refuge in the "last instance" that is yet to come in its paja-
mas down from an apartment to the street. Instead, today
is a time to assess the roles of critique and imagine modes of
criticality in relation to what Luc Boltanski and Eve Chiapello describe as "the new spirit of capitalism," particularly
as this spirit is materializing locally (in whatever "local"
one may be in!).

In what I'm characterizing as the post-euphoric moment of neoliberalism, forms of critique that have historically been in the wheelhouse of left critique are now
brought into an out-of-kilter dialectic with capitalism itself.
Boltanski and Chiapello map this dialectic in the spirited
reformation of capitalism from May 1968 to today in relation to "the rhetoric of critique." They compellingly lay out
a dialectical relationship between the focus of two modes
of critique—social critique and artistic critique—and the
ways in which capitalism has transformed itself by responding to and absorbing the very aspects of these modes
of critique that were to burst us out of the reproduction of
inequity and alienation. Artistic critique, as Boltanski and
Chiapello outline it, is a deeply affective critique of the in-
completeness of everyday life, of the stifling of the potential
of life by the relations of capitalism, the sway of the state,
the containment of city life and the life of the streets, and
the relationships between people. The keyword for artistic critique is *alienation,* and it has historically sought to
outflank new forms of such social (and soul) displacement
as they cohere in the city, in the domestic sphere, and in
all affective relations. At the same time, new management
language and practices have adapted to dampen the effects
of this critique and to *give the appearance of* new solutions to
the old question of alienation within the relations of capitalist production: this, to a degree, has sought to "disarm"
critique. This leads Boltanski and Chiapello to pose the

question: *Must we not instead start from different bases—that is to say, ask if the forms of capitalism which have developed over the last thirty years, while incorporating whole sections of the artistic critique and subordinating it to profit-making, have not emptied the demands for liberation and authenticity of what gave them substance, and anchored them in people's everyday experience?*[4]

Cultural critique and art criticism, then, whether they use art and art institutions or the social as their entry point, face a similar question: How to produce new publics and how to forge non-absorbable forms of critique that will allow us to take aim, take time, take space, and take collectivized pleasure in order to grab the present moment by the hand and lead it to the language of less arrogant forms of social reproduction? That is, what form of critique is forged by reflection and necessity in this dialectic of absorption, accommodation, and (ironically) non-transformation? Today we are caught in a moment desperate to reproduce itself despite its hollow slogans: "there is no such thing as society," "beneath the paving stones, real estate," or the sleep-deprived chant that "the market will correct itself." How are critique and art criticism placed within this process of reproduction?

Two

In his lecture for *Judgment and Contemporary Art Criticism*, Tirdad Zolghadr outlined a relationship between criticism, critique, and criticality, with the last being an inward reflexive turn. I wonder if we can locate this inward turn as a symptom of the mediations that neoliberalism brings to bear on cultural critique and art criticism? This turn could indicate a rescaling or containment of what commentators across the board define as a social and economic crisis to the cultural field. If this inward turn is such a containment, then, rather than an attempt to build a language of critique that can grabble with the uneven experience of the social today, we see critique caught in the swirling, yet pleasingly warm, pool of the new spirit of capitalism—accentuating individual consumptive and aesthetic experiences that spring from art situated firmly in a cultural sphere sure of itself. On the one hand, this surrenders the purpose of artistic critique in the manner that Boltanski and Chiapello define it, and on the other hand, it allows a focused examination of art criticism as a definable field and practice. But what type of literacy—if we conceive of literacy as a remaking rather than an expertise, in the manner that Richard Hoggart and Gayatri Spivak do—is art criticism making? In other words, a crisis that turns inward to locate itself—in art criticism, or in another field—risks missing the crisis outside itself. It misses being a part of the crisis by generating its own! And then it can take a detour around the central aspect of critique—the thrilling articulation of the aesthetic to the social and startling joining of the possibilities of art to the structures and mediations of life.

What possibilities do we have at hand, in our globalized-local, in our public-private neighbourhood of "the ownership society," or, conversely, what possibilities do we have in our counter-collectives or in our affective alliances of everyday life? Let me use two tendencies in the critical practices of two other participants in the forum—Maria Fusco and Diedrich Diederichsen—to frame the possibilities we have had historically and how they may crystallize as critique today. Firstly, I would identify interdisciplinarity as an operative mode, not as an institutional mode of organizing, but as a mode of thinking and writing that compounds and overlaps other possibilities of thought. Secondly, there is an expansion of the cultural field through "art writing" or a poetics of critical engagement that extends not only into narrative modes of critique, but also into an expanded field of cultural practices focused through the eye of art writing. This approach relates to both the art object and the institution, but also the form of art criticism as an institution itself: too often taken as a formally transparent or static practice (partly due to its relationship to the promotion of art, as Sven Lütticken argues) and often unquestioned in its function to create value for artists and artworks, art criticism can calcify through a bland trust in the representational function of language.[5]

The "personism" (poet and art writer Frank O'Hara's term[6]) that is often called in to rescue the art review and give it value as an experience in itself—both de-skilling the article and adding a dollop of taste culture—continues to take the architecture of meaning for granted. Even with an expansive and compelling personism in which we may recognize our own affiliations and affections, such criticism does not yield the experience of a text in that it is not a parallel engagement with the making of meaning—the art text is never allowed to be in excess of meaning and is harnessed to a language of representation within the strictures of description and evaluation. To pick up on another point from Tirdad Zolghadr's paper, the incommensurability of the art object is only a referential aspect of the art text.

This present volume questions the limitations and temporality of criticism—that is, the time that criticism and judgment build. Much of the reflection of the critics in this volume cuts across the language of crisis within the discipline of art criticism to provide some positions within a texture of research, knowledge, necessity, and critique for the present moment. If we feel overly constricted by such a moment, or even overwhelmed by mediations that bear down with the force of commonsense or coherent and fully armoured logics, Henri Lefebvre reminds us that "Events belie forecasts: to the extent that events are historical, they upset calculations."[7] This imagination of time and agency as event, history, and upset calculations seems to be a fertile construct for cultural criticism and art writing: historical, present, and yet overturning calculations.

1. Neil Smith, "Toxic Capitalism," *New Political Economy* 14, no. 3 (2009), 407–12.

2. Raymond Williams, *The Long Revolution* (New York: Harper Torchbooks, 1961), 46.

3. Leslie Sklair, *The Transnational Capitalist Class* (Oxford: Blackwell, 2001).

4. Luc Boltanski and Eve Chiapello, *The New Spirit of Capitalism*, trans. Gregory Elliott (London: Verso, 2005), 420.

5. Sven Lütticken, *Secret Publicity: Essays on Contemporary Art* (Rotterdam: NAi Publishers, 2005).

6. "Personism" was a short statement on poetics that O'Hara contributed to the groundbreaking anthology *Poetics of the New American Poetry*, eds. Donald Allen and Warren Tallman (New York: Grove Press, 1973). As a poetics, "personism" was a defining feature of the New York School poets. For an extended reading of O'Hara and his relation to visual art, see Lytle Shaw, *The Poetics of Coterie* (Iowa City: The University of Iowa Press, 2006).

7. Henri Lefebvre, *Explosion: Marxism and the French Revolution*, trans. Alfred Ehrenfeld (New York: Monthly Review Press, 1969), 7.

*Forum Discussion Transcripts with
Prefatory Remarks by Kristina Lee Podesva*

Kristina Lee Podesva

Between the Question Mark
and the Comma

In thinking about how criticism operates, I stumbled upon a conceptual space lying somewhere between the question mark and the comma. It happened through simple editorial observation: I noted how many authors in *Fillip* 6, which took on the theme of education in response to documenta XII's third leitmotif, tended to bracket their texts with questions and lists, suggesting that interrogation provides a convenient starting point while lists supply us not with clear, concrete answers, but rather with links in a continual chain of considerations.

Questions and interrogation, of course, are not sparkling new devices we deploy in search of greater knowledge. They have been used over and over again in writing, art, and writing about art in support of inquiry, debate, provocation, and that old, familiar Hegelian "three-step" known as the dialectic (described by Tirdad Zolghadr). Questions are not new, and, moreover, they are not neutral for they can, in many respects, act as disguises for the predetermined or as apertures masking closures. Nevertheless, they *do* actively begin things, directing us toward a space that we can build in conversation with a relatively more open, or at the very least, curious attitude. I wholeheartedly disagree with Gertrude Stein's conclusion that the question mark is the "completely most uninteresting" form of punctuation, an unnecessary symbol that "pleases neither the eye nor the ear" and redundantly announces the obvious.[1] Instead, the question mark occasions a productive shift, however molecular, in the mind of a reader, prompting us to think more about what is unknown rather than what is known, preparing us for uncertainty although we seek clarity.

In the best case scenario, art criticism stimulates

conversations on contemporary art that proceed forward in a generative fashion, where articulations veer away from final pronouncements and lean more toward a kind of ongoing grappling, or an inductive process (à la Maria Fusco's suggestion) that, nonetheless, may pause along the way to stake something worth wrangling over; inevitably, though, this process compels us to pick up again where someone else had left off. The underlying aporia somehow manages, in varying degrees, to position best-case scenario criticism in such a way that the forms and functions of art and of criticism simultaneously open up, rather than shrink, with every new temporal and spatial circumstance introduced. Today, more often than not, criticism appears sandwiched in between the advertorial content of glossy gallery and fashion spreads, where the occasional, engaging essay or review exists to support the business of art rather than the other way around. Here, criticism is complicit in the art-magazine-as-shopping-catalogue phenomena, or even the art-magazine-as-teen-zine, reduxing the top ten lists of yesteryear found in *Bop* or *Tiger Beat*, only now Jonathan Meese and Takashi Murakami have replaced Ricky Schroeder and Corey Haim as the idols of our moment and attention.

But, to return to the possibilities of criticism and its speculative grammar, I'd like to consider more carefully and fully the comma. It is perhaps the punctuation mark most suited to a forum in which public debate and engagement occurs, and where a non-hierarchical variety of voices and a diversity of topics take up residence. It is also, on the textual level, an abstract representation of seriality (where lists can indicate a sequence), of collectivity and inclusion (where groups of ideas and objects are linked), of contingency (where independent and dependent clauses connect and individual iterations hinge upon others), of apposition (where definitions derive from juxtapositions), and of movement (where a syncopated rhythm takes shape that both cleaves and binds adjacent parts in a forward sweep). Moreover, the comma provides a space to pause, offering a placeholder in whichever moment, expressed alternately as a series of perpetual nows that discourage or unmoor the static and the finite. It is finally the comma that initiates dialogue and ushers in the verbal address, declaring and distributing a space between speakers, listeners, givers, and receivers.[2]

Can we put forth a grammar for criticism that makes more translucent the opaque skin covering art and shrouding the countless ways in which our perspectives and positions are interconnected through time, geography, knowledge, taste, and so on? Can we actualize a critical engagement with art that reflects back to us what we are, or at least what we think we are, and yet contests that knowledge, and perpetually obliges us to re-tool it? Can we compose a criticism that illuminates the edges of things, of distantly related points that stretch out radially into the deep, dark space of the yet-to-be? It is, perhaps, only in a long list of things (separated by commas) that declare or plague or drone on that we find a place worth occupying.

For me, this space between the question mark and the comma is, for now, where I'd like to locate and advocate for a particular and productive brand of criticism. It's an open and vast space with room enough for all kinds of maneuvering. Whether it is built by catalyzing discussions through the act of questioning or by making multiple small inroads connected in conversation via the comma, it does not matter because ultimately it's the thought behind it that counts.

1. See Kenneth Goldsmith, *Gertrude Stein on Punctuation* (Jersey City: Abaton Books, 2000).
2. See Irit Rogoff, "Smuggling: An Embodied Criticality," (2006), available at http://eipcp.net/dlfiles/rogoff-smuggling.

<u>February 27, 2009</u>
Keynote Address
Tirdad Zolghadr

<u>Tonik Wojtyra</u>: I think it was Tobias Meyer from Sotheby's who, at some point during the art market splendor, was asinine enough to say that good art is the most expensive art. [Tobias Meyer was quoted as saying, "The best art is the most expensive because the market is so smart," in Sarah Thornton, "Love and Money," *Artforum: Scene and Herd*, May 11, 2006: http://artforum.com/diary/id=10968.] If the art market is so smart, based on his expert opinion, then what, in your expert opinion, is the best art writing? [laughter]

<u>Tirdad Zolghadr</u>: It's a good question because, as I was trying to suggest earlier, the agendas between the art writers and the artists are not the same. There are artworks that bring out the best in writers and artworks that do the opposite. There are artworks that prompt a flurry of critical karaoke and then there are artworks that push the writer to reconsider knee-jerk topographies.

<u>Diedrich Diederichsen</u>: What [Tobias Meyer] is saying is that there is judgment taking place, and the art market uses this kind of judgment. If there is such a narrow connection between art writing and judgment, maybe the crisis of judgment and the hope of art writing are not so closely connected. But maybe it's not the art market that's responsible for that. [Art writing] cannot exist without opposing the other forces that produce judgment all the time, like audiences, markets, artists....

<u>Tirdad Zolghadr</u>: So what you are saying is that the relationship between judgment and art writing is perhaps tenuous and that perhaps criticism offers the possibility of standing against the kind of judgment that is pursued in other fields so rigorously, such as within the art market. So that criticism is inherently opposing judgment as opposed to pursuing it.

<u>Diedrich Diederichsen</u>: The last thing that I would like to suggest is that maybe because all these other types of judgment are happening, art writing (although it could do other things than judging) has to become the superior judgment.

<u>Tirdad Zolghadr</u>: So the fact that judgment is being pursued so resolutely in these other fields is an opportunity for criticism to engage in judgment in a more subtle matter.

<u>Diedrich Diederichsen</u>: Not necessarily. [laughter]

<u>Tirdad Zolghadr</u>: I'm just paraphrasing here! [laughs]

<u>Diedrich Diederichsen</u>: My point would be that art writing, in its shortcomings and opportunities and so on, is not closely connected for any intrinsic reason to judgment except in a very distant echo. But [art writing] is placed—not so much in an ethical sense but in the contemporary context—in a context with other constantly judging forces. There it inherits the obligation to produce something that competes with, or argues against, these other forms of judgment that exist.

Tirdad Zolghadr: Again to para-phrase for the audience in the back: Criticism does not inherently fulfill this role of judgment except by way of a very faint reminiscence of Kant. But the way that it is placed and contextualized places it under pressure to perform judgment in some form or another.

Mohammad Salemy: You brilliantly explain the whole drama, but today the very fact that somebody writes [about] you is the judgment. You don't even have to read the essay. It's like you pull out the catalogue and just the fact that you were written about is the judgment. Just the fact that you were included in the show or not is the judgment. The judgment is already made pre-writing. I recently read a very opinionated piece of art criticism in the *New York Times* which was shockingly, completely judgmental, and I was like, "Wow, I can't believe the critic, [Ken] Johnson, can go so deep into questioning the motives of the artist, questioning the aesthetics of the work, questioning everything about the piece!" [See Ken Johnson, "Material for a Palestinian's Life and Death," *New York Times*, February 12, 2009, http://nytimes.com/2009/02/13/arts/design/13jaci.html.] Everything seems fine until you find out that the show is Emily Jacir's at the Guggenheim. It was basically a political judgment on the validity of the Palestinian struggle put in the form of [a review of] Emily's work. The point is that [the] Hugo Boss [Prize] particularly picked Emily. That is a judgment, too.

Diedrich Diederichsen: That's a mix of two things: Consequentiality (things with consequence) and judgment. Judgments don't necessarily have consequences. Judgments are just making a clear statement about something. But when you say that even being included in the catalogue is a judgment, then there is some act of consequentiality, some act with a consequence. A judgment is an act that has a possible consequence, that asks for a consequence—one that is specific and different from other acts of consequence because, in the best case, it makes its criteria explicit and can be discussed, just like you can debate this review in the *New York Times* because it is judgmental. I think that's the difference.

Audience member: Can I ask you to maybe indulge in a little "futurology"? Can you predict what might happen with art writing over the next, say, decade? What do you think might come after visual culture? Do you think that art writing might be the thing that creates a relationship between critical theory and curatorial practices, and how do you think that might unfold within a kind of institution?

Tirdad Zolghadr: I'm not very good at this kind of thing.... I can tell you what I'm worried might happen. I can refer to the "neck verse," this epistemic free flow, the possibility to engage in plural disciplinarity with impunity. In literary studies, the neck verse is often mentioned as a kind of parable of literacy and power. In the Middle Ages, the neck verse was the verse that clergymen could read from the bible to prove that they could read, and this would prove that they were clergymen, and this would exempt them from any punishment before the law. They could get away with murder, literally, if they could prove that they were clergymen. And they would sit in front of the judge, and they would read this verse, and the judge would say, "You can go home now, you're obviously a clergyman." The problem was that it was always the same verse, so people would just memorize it and be sent home rather than be hung from the nearest tree. It's a very useful parable when it comes to this carte blanche that I keep referring to, because it's about this kind of mystified and mystifiable rationalization of certain privileges of a professional creed. It's also a question of an institutionalized form of forgery and about class privileges and so on and so forth. So this situation, this neck verse, where you have curators and artists and critics engaging with different theories of globalization and discussions of the history of philosophy and the history of political philosophy with such enthusiasm and unchecked vigor.... I mean, the number of panels I've been introduced to where I have absolutely nothing to say—Leninism, the early history of Christian philosophy, Arab migrants, and on and on—is pretty impressive. And all I'd have to do is sit there and do the arty mystery thing, because I'm the token critic/curator—critter—on the panel. I do have a feeling that this situation will possibly lead to a backlash that will temporarily give the Kantians, so to speak, the upper hand. I do think that there has already been a reaction to the internationalism that was so aggressively espoused over the last ten years by postcolonially informed curators, writers, and artists because so much of it was based on vaguely intellectualized wishful thinking or on barely justified combinations of various theoretical statements which did very little for the understanding of how internationalism really does work between the first world and

third world contexts—the violence that does occur when things try to travel from A to B. Nor did it help much when it came to understanding or discussing the art. When I talk about trying to define some sort of specificity, it's not so much a call to order, it's not so much a yearning for some sort of canon or method or clearly recognizable history that we can all agree on. It's simply trying to reintroduce the question of whether there are places where we can reasonably be expected to shut up, because we tend to do more harm than good, more often than not.

Kelly Lycan: It made me think a little about the point you were making in the second dilemma which was that there is no place that an art writer can commit to their depth, and I wondered if you could elaborate on that specifically in terms of the critic and curator.

Tirdad Zolghadr: I am indebted to Gayatri Charkravorty Spivak's take… concerned with the ease with which those who speak can weasel their way out of responsibility. There are those who speak for the object (the artist) or those who step back and say this object can speak for itself. Spivak's essay suggests both. One of the obstacles for those who try to ventriloquize the object of their discourse is that this notion [assumes] that there's a level playing field, that theory is simply a box of tools just like a wrench and a hammer, and that it does not inflict violence. Yet the very etymological root of "theory" points to an ancient Greek context where the Theorian were opposed not to practice but to asepsis, where the asepsis was an individual opinion that anyone was capable of—a slave, a child. So there's a question of the privilege to narrate. If you take these things into consideration, it's quite easy to see that there's an ethics of criticism that takes into account the limits of criticism and the limits of things on which you can reasonably be expected to have an opinion in a professional context; [this] is more than just a question of refinement or good taste, it's also political or ethical.

Audience member: If it's fair to say that art criticism and judgment are somehow related to the production of art, then is it incumbent upon artists to undertake value judgments from within their work?

Tirdad Zolghadr: I wouldn't see why not. As I've been trying to point out, I don't think that there is an intrinsic problem between artists engaging in what critics are expected to engage in. But when this happens, it is not a question of two agendas coming closer to one another, but rather, in many cases, professional desperation. At one point, there was a desperate shortage of images with respect to writing. But the situation is now vice versa, so now you have more artists engaging in what you are describing. [Boris] Groys would probably say that to assume that there's a level playing field just because there are some artists who have the permission to engage in this activity is like saying that you don't need unions because you have the lottery. It's still very much skewed….

Holly Ward: Going back to the ethics of criticism…. I recently saw Jan Verwoert speak in Berlin at the United Nations Plaza about his own role as critic. He seemed to display a sense of shame about the reprehensible act of producing criticism and this horrible kind of identity that he seemed to have forged for himself as a critic. I'm curious to see how you might describe your feelings about the act of criticism.

Tirdad Zolghadr: Were you at the second night or the first?

Holly Ward: The first night.

Tirdad Zolghadr: The question is referring to Jan Verwoert's series of talks "Why are conceptual artists painting again? Because they think it's a good idea" at the Building (formerly known as the United Nations Plaza) in Berlin. It is a talk where he does have a very apologetic position as a critic; where the act of naming, the authoritative gesture that is associated with criticism is repeatedly brought to the fore and then repeatedly deconstructed. I asked you if you were there for the first night or the second night because the first night I did try to gently poke fun at Jan Verwoert during the Q and A. I said that it was ironic that someone who so eloquently names and deconstructs and disparages entire art practices of certain generations with such Greenbergian majesty would then continuously step back and do these pirouettes of auto-deconstruction and disavow the role of the critic as king-maker. And I was actually arguing that I would much prefer less denegation and more living up to this, the Theorian aspect of things. If you do have this rhetorical thrust that is going to cast shades of black and white and pit people against each other, I actually don't have a particular problem with it as long as it is ideologically grounded with a reasonable measure of self-reflexivity. I much prefer [this position] because it can be the beginning of a healthy argument, and it can be a lot more rewarding than the weak politicality of the paradox that I was describing before.

Jeff Derksen: I just had a brief speculative question to pick up on the weak politics of the paradox, and also the nice term that you mentioned that you and Polly Staple were using: "binary fluffing." Is binary fluffing the cultural logic of post-Fordism?

Tirdad Zolghadr: Is binary fluffing the cultural logic of post-Fordism? Sounds like the beginning of an essay…[laughter] Thanks. [more laughter] It's what I was trying to suggest less articulately than the way you just put it. But yes, absolutely. I did try to suggest that this comfortable posing of *seeming* opposites [is a way] to keep things in suspension without having to take any clear position. On the one hand, I don't think it's a problem. The only problem with it is that it comes so naturally to us. I don't see any alternative to it right now. I think its always nice to pick a fight like Claire Bishop does, or like the way I wish Jan Verwoert would do now and then, but at the end of the day, this is the way we have been reared ideologically: to persistently pursue this weak politicality. It does have something to do with the post-Fordist context. We are educated to constantly be open to some other opinion or truth which could pop up at any time. You are supposed to be flexible, sociable, and generally charming enough to be able to integrate this new truth into your intellectual positioning in some form or another. So, yes, I would agree. [laughter, applause]

<u>February 28, 2009</u>
Panel One
Panelists: Kristina Lee Podesva,
Tom Morton, and William Wood
Moderator: John O'Brian

<u>Kristina Lee Podesva</u>: I'm sitting here as a representative of *Fillip* in a sense, but also as an artist and a writer, and perhaps to represent a divergent view from what Tom [Morton] articulated just now in his paper. Instead of being interested in these intimate relationships—these intimacies that he discussed—I'm actually really quite interested, more so, in what art and criticism can share. To me, that interest lies in the fact that both require a public audience, and their engagement with one another occurs in an actually public context. Returning to Sven Lütticken, who writes about critics who lament their instrumentalization by the "real decision-makers—the collectors, curators, and gallery owners." [See Sven Lütticken, *Secret Publicity: Essays on Contemporary Art* (Rotterdam: NAi Publishers, 2005), 7.] For him, their complaints about the service role they occupy in the production of art-critical sales talk belie a failure to see how this view inhabits a rather small and inconsequential domain, delimited by what he calls "professional pride and privileges." Instead, Lütticken offers the critic a meaningful alternative to consider "the potential of art to constitute a critical form of publicness within the contemporary spectacle." If the artist renders certain phenomena and questions knowable or visible in public, the critic then, perhaps, makes that endeavor legible and legitimate, sometimes in alignment with the artist's intentions, but at other times not. Still, both the artist

and the critic make their cases in public and to various publics. By public, I realize that we have a term equally as elusive as criticism. Michael Warner has gone far to attempt to grasp the notion of the public in his book *Publics and Counterpublics* (2005), observing that publics are multiple and mutable, echoing perhaps [Michel] Foucault's project on power. The point of Warner's study of publics is that they "exist only by virtue of their imagining. They are a kind of fiction that has taken on a life, and very potent life at that, and that when publics are addressed there is a struggle engaged at varying levels of salience to consciousness, from calculated tactic to mute cognitive noise over the conditions that bring them together as a public." [See Michael Warner, *Publics and Counterpublics* (New York: Zone Books, 2005), 8.] To identify a public, Warner recommends that we discern whom is being addressed and how. Publics are, therefore, in Warner's study, "essentially intertextual, frameworks for understanding texts against an organized background of the circulation of other texts," [See Warner, 15] which are, in our world, increasingly images.

And so, Warner essentially brings us to the notion that publics are highly unstable and, thus, counterpublics offered by the artist and even the critic, among others, can put into circulation new engagements through their practices, and in the best case scenario this manifests in a kind of "poetic world-making." [See Warner, 114.]

So, in relation to art and criticism today, I'm concerned that this word "crisis" is the word to which we continually return, because I feel that if we are frustrated or even alarmed by criticism circulating as is, it means we do not like what is being said because we do not identify with the publics being addressed. Faced with this fact, I think we have two choices, either to find the publics we seek or to create them. These are questions of distribution and production. Of course, practical dilemmas arise here, the first being how do we find our publics when criticism and writing about art is de-centered, multiple, and so voluminous? We therefore need filters to wade through this vast sea of content. And, in relation to producing the publics we seek, we must consider how to do this when resources are limited. In some cases, as Tom mentioned, we have the question of time, Perhaps *Fillip* represents the antithesis to the art diary or the art fair or the art blog, because we're not even published monthly, we're not even published quarterly, we're published three times a year, so perhaps we're giving a bit of time to folk to consider what they are going to discuss. And then, of course, in terms of space, there's the 750-word review typical of most magazines and, of course, at *Fillip* we try to make that 1500 words. So, there is this question of time and space, but how do you do [criticism] with limited resources?

One of the things that I noticed in the *October* round table, in the discussion packet [*Supplement for Judgment and Contemporary Art Criticism*], is that Helen Molesworth says that good criticism is what artists read. But, faced with this multiple number of publics, I'm sort of asking this question: which artists, which critics, which publics? I'd say that one of the roles I think *Fillip* is really trying to take on is this notion

of creating these publics, and a place to start new discussions, and to change, therefore, the number of publics that we currently see in operation, and to distribute that information as well. Those are just a couple of questions that I have that I'd like to open for discussion: producing these new publics through criticism and how to distribute the information that we create through these new publics. I think that's one of the greatest challenges of our time: how to find them.

John O'Brian: I'm trying to draw connections between Tirdad's talk last night, Bill's talk on the left, Tom's on the right—and those aren't judgments about political positions. [laughter] I was very much struck that in Tirdad's talk he kept coming back to dance as a metaphor. You certainly were engaged in a critical foxtrot, like Adorno, as you put it, in terms of discussing questions of negation and denegation of judgment, or what Bill calls exclusive judgment—in other words, totalizations. You were performing a pirouette that at moments seemed to go out of control and then righted itself. So the messy pluralities that you discuss were present in your talk, I thought, in terms of the elegant quotation, the refusal to totalize, and adding up to something in the end, which was the judgment that negation was something to be watched out for. The processes of denegation are ones that we need to be talking about because they indicate that—as the forum's workbook shows—other directions are being taken. I was struck as I read through this [the workbook] last night by how much [Clement] Greenberg figures in it, though Greenberg hasn't figured much in discussions today. The workbook makes me pleased, because when I did work as an art historian on Greenberg, I did it so we could read Greenberg whole. What we had before the collected works were *Art and Culture* and a couple of other canonical articles that were always trotted out. In 1980, I was sitting in Widener Library in Cambridge, Massachusetts, trying to make sense of why the canon had hardened. I thought we should have Greenberg—this is the art historian speaking—the Good, the Bad, and the Ugly, that we could read whole. And it was my great disappointment in meeting artists later in Canada and the United States that they hadn't even read Greenberg the first time around, particularly painters. They had had him in their studios and that had been the connection. It was the intimacy that counted for them, rather than the sometimes contradictory critical judgments of Greenberg. I think of Greenberg as something like the sanctified ur-modernist artist of British Columbia, Emily Carr. The sanctified ur-critic, as presented by the people writing here [in the workbook], isn't [John] Ruskin, who is profoundly moral in his writing, nor [Charles] Baudelaire, who goes somewhere else with criticism. It is Greenberg, the sanctified and vilified ur-critic, the sort of originary critical figure in North America that comes to attention at the very moment the United States gains economic power following the Second World War (that is, a kind of exclusionary economic and military power following the Second World War). That made him read in the first place and that made it necessary for the sanctified view of him to be undone. The process of undoing that view—and here's where, as an art historian looking back on histories of criticism, I am interested in the process—by, say, Rosalind Krauss, who was once a Greenbergian, by [Benjamin] Buchloch, by [Douglas] Crimp, indeed by others sitting in this room who have brilliantly insisted on refusing the totalizing— the magisterial, as you said, Tirdad— pronouncements of Greenberg, needs close attention. In the process of negating his judgments against the attempt now to denegate them, Greenberg got reestablished again. In other words, in the process of his work being undone it became necessary to read him all over again. You couldn't understand what was happening in postmodernist and poststructuralist discourse in New York without re-reading Greenberg, if you were going to be serious in thinking about what Krauss, Crimp, Buchloch, and others had to say.

I was glad, Bill, that you brought up the subject of institutional critique, because that's on the agenda here. This is absolutely central to what we are talking about. We are all within the habitus, the social field of art. That social field is a frame, percep-tual and mental as much as it is physical. Institutional critique came out of the critique of institutions and is precisely the requirement for self-reflexivity about the institution that we all participate in. [John] Berger had interesting things to say about this. I think Andrea Fraser's article from 2005 in *Artforum* is the best single account of it because she lays out a particular history of how that occurred from a position of *parti pris*. "I may have given the term insti-tutional critique currency," Fraser states, in this way writing herself into the history and reflecting on the kind of biases that may be involved there. Criticism as a practice is nothing if not engaged in the institution of art, within the habitus, within the frame. At its best, criticism is always going to refuse those totalizations. It's going to recognize the messiness of projects, the range of art, the different voices that have been used, the possibility of other interpretations. Of course, what was particularly horrific about the late Greenberg were the critical exclusions. They were based, however, on theories about the social arrangements of capitalism, ones we should still pay close attention to because they are still with us, even though they have become more transnational. The refusal of the negation of judgment, the denegations that have been presented by the three of you [Tom Morton, Kristina Lee Podesva, William Wood], seems like a good place from which to continue the discussion.

Audience member: What can art criticism—in its various forms—learn from music and architectural criticism? And how does the criticism of time-based and static work differ?

William Wood: Well, it's fundamentally questions of competence. I mean, I like music, I know what I like. When people say "I don't know much about art but I know what I like," I come back and say that "I don't know much about chemistry but I know what I like." [laughter] I spend a lot of time looking at visual art and working with the structures of visual art, so I really can't talk that well about other forms [of art]. There are other people, such as Diedrich, here who do, who can, write about many forms well, and that's a remarkable thing to do. Regarding time-based work: Obviously music and some forms of theater and film and so on can be seen iteratively over a longer period of time than

works of art in the form of exhibitions. And that's a limitation. That's one of the traditional limits of art criticism—that it's a report on an ephemeral situation and event. In terms of static and time based, I don't think that we encounter images in those forms anymore. They are sort of mixed up in some way; static images seem to be implicated in moving and moving in static (except for how long can you stand to watch the piece and whether there are limits to your ability to do that). But there are also artists who have played very much with that. You cannot experience the whole work (Boris Groys goes into this) because you just do not have the time. And it's constructed to be a kind of monumental thing that's beyond comprehension. That's my answer to the question.

Tom Morton: What I have to add in terms of static and time-based media? I absolutely agree with Bill that these distinctions aren't so useful. But apart from, if one is writing a review in a very small number of words, accounting for the absence of a work, the evocation of it can almost be the whole review (there [might] be nothing apart from describing what's going on in an artist's film). So there are questions, in terms of that short form of criticism, there's part of it that is evocation, and there are questions of balance with that, and some form of kind of thinking of the thing evoked, and possibly judgments somewhere along the way. So there is some difference, but to some degree it's practical.

Kristina Lee Podesva: Well, I just wanted to return to this point about competencies in criticism. When I think about this, I tend to think about

Marcel Broodthaers's *Interview with a Cat* from 1970. Of course, that came out of the project where he, I believe, was in Düsseldorf in the basement putting on his institutional critique projects and dealing with the museum. And what he's doing is asking a cat various esoteric questions about art, and the cat only responds by "meowing" over and over and over again. And he comes to the point where he asks, "what do you think of this, what should we do, should we close the museum?" And the cat just responds, "meow." But I think what he's pointing to is the context of the museum and the context of criticism often can legitimate it, and you don't have to have any competencies. I'm not saying that's a good thing, but I'm just saying that the context can very well legitimate all kinds of gibberish, and with the understanding that there is some kind of competency behind it. But I don't know how much that's always the case. That's all I would offer.

Diedrich Diederichsen: Yes, I wanted to support Tom's mentioning of the intimacy of judgment. But maybe it's not so helpful to think of this idea of the intention of judgment in terms of the professional procedure of criticism, but that it is a key element of reception. It's an element of reception of every type of audience or recipient: positioning yourself towards whatever object or project or process you are getting involved with [and] how you think of it in terms of value. And I think this has a lot to do with time and the time-based-ness of your engagement. It's a direct comparison between what else you could do in that moment with your very precious lifetime. It's not such a rationalized, instrumentalist procedure, but it's something that

happens intuitively and constantly, all the time—it's getting revised all the time. But those are judgments, and they are very intimate; they are not necessarily visible or on hand in [the] critical process, but I think that without them there wouldn't be anything happening.

I wanted to contradict Tom when he was saying that art criticism is not well paid. Of course, it could be paid better—I wouldn't mind that—but it's paid much better than any other form of criticism in culture. That is maybe one of the reasons why people are so reluctant to not make any judgments, because they would possibly loose the position to be able to continue receiving this kind of money.

And the third thing I wanted to say was about the end of art or the past-ness in art. Maybe that has something to do intrinsically with the idea of autonomy—that autonomy has something to do with the fact that there is no immediate connection between what you are doing in art and the outside world. You're not immediately influencing it; you're influencing it symbolically, or whatever. We don't have to go into that…. But this has, of course, always, this "as if" aspect. It has to do with the fact that if it's "as if" now, that it must have been immediately in the past. It's taken as though its notion refers to some past model of where the "if" was located. And I think because of that, because of that "as if"-ness, that it's always using that idea of the way we deal with things of art was once the modus operandi in daily life, that the judgment of value vis-à-vis this situation is the maybe desperate but somewhat legitimate attempt to (without any success) to reconstruct this past.

John O'Brian: Yes, "as if." I read [Arthur] Danto and I think that someone must have hit him over the head with a Brillo box, because everything is before the Brillo box and after. He is constructing it "as if" before. There's an immediate, huge rupture that then occurs after.

Antonia Hirsch: What I suddenly remembered while I was listening to Tom were the reviews that Donald Judd used to write for *Artforum* or *Art in America*. I remember seeing those for the first time, and they basically made me laugh out loud, they are so amazingly blunt and opinionated. He was actually nixed from that particular reviewing job because they were so opinionated. And I'm wondering if maybe he was ahead of his time and just thinking that if there has been a move away from this tendency or this function of judgment, perhaps, in the postmodern moment, and now at a time where the public sphere doesn't seem to occur so effectively anymore in the print media. Maybe the role of the critic is to have an opinion, not to pass an authoritative judgment, but to have an opinion that will result in a discourse that happens elsewhere. And so, that's maybe one question— is that maybe the case? And the other would be: Where does this discourse then take place? Is the reason we have had such a proliferation of these school models (like UNP, symposia, and so on) where the real criticism now takes place that we don't actually get it in the magazines anymore?

William Wood: I would say that Judd is a figure that would be placed at exactly that area I was indicating between the judgment of objects or of works and the judgment of projects. Because, if you do read his reviews, they are blunt or full of judgment. They are very, well, funny. He sort of says, "last year so and so showed this work and this year, well, it wasn't as good," and that's sort of a judgment I guess, but it's shaky; he uses very qualitative terms. Maybe this relates back to what Diedrich was saying, too, that maybe the school models exist again in that "as if" way, "as if" this time we can learn something, "as if" this time we can actually go back and start and rethink our positions.

Kristina Lee Podesva: I think that one of the things that you're pointing to, Antonia, is not only a lack of public space in the print world, but I think also in the physical world. I think perhaps that is a reason why the school forms have developed—as a way to create space that people can use to confer together and to check with one another and to have a kind of exchange. But I'm also wondering about the formatting of reviews. You have a maximum word limit; you're only given so much time and space to consider things. Perhaps also the school form is another way to get more in depth, to have a little more time to talk about these things. And also there's in a sense no accountability. So with criticism, once you've published it, it goes into the public record, then there's the accountability of other critics or artists to contest what you say. In a way, that level of speculation in discourse, and actually sitting down and talking to people, allows things to get worked out without any kind of penalty. Once you put it in print form, you could be penalized because people could disagree with you publicly, but also it could mean that you won't get another writing job, or something like that. But in a sense there's this level of penalty.

Antonia Hirsch: I would actually disagree with that. Because yes, there is the possibility of losing a job, but usually your public is so far away from you when you publish that you may never have that correlation of your opinion and words. Because, as we have it right now, we have a very delayed response rather than actually having to answer the criticism right away. There is actually a dialogue where things get hashed out and you have to justify why you said what you said. Whereas print media is so removed that somebody might not want to talk to you at a party, but...

Tom Morton: I think there are certain penalties that are involved in the school model as well. There are certain pieties that, if they are not observed, become socially difficult. School models really do tend to be rather kind of formalized version of discussions that are for private view anyway. I mean, one of the things for a project like Manifesta 6 was that there wasn't funding to bring people outside of a certain golden circle. So it became that a wide social group was taken from one part of the world to another. And while they seem sort of super open and free, these things are really a lot less accessible than a traditional review in a fairly traditional art magazine.

I'm kind of interested in this. There may be examples which I don't know about, but perhaps the Internet is a useful space for this kind of thing. At *frieze* we have a comment section, which is moderated (or else you get these "LOL, yeah, screw you guys la la la la"), and that comment section

has actually had some interesting discussions about criticism, from artists as well as others. I think that's something that has actually been missing in this discussion: how artists use criticism. If you get a great review, that's great; you get a bad review, that's awful—or whether it's something that informs artistic practice. It would be interesting to hear [from] any artists in the audience....

Kristina Lee Podesva: The Internet forums, are they anonymized?

Tom Morton: No, there's no way to do that. The convention is that one uses one's name. And if one doesn't want to do that, I guess it is impossible to impel someone to do so.

John Luna: I'm a studio teacher, and I wanted to address some of this discussion around schooling. Kristina, I was really interested in this discussion you talked about and this disjuncture between poetics and the need to talk about an audience. Also, I think that it was really poignant what you said, Tom, about contingency and time and feeling the voice at your elbow. Because to me, the very factual consequence of dealing openly with students and I think, a sort of student consensus, which every art teacher fears, that there is judgment without analysis. You know, the dirty rumor of an art school is that there's a lot of judgment taking place but not a lot of analysis; the apparatus hasn't been clear. I wanted to ask myself if this could possibly be good, to see the critical faculty of judgment as being something akin to what the artist Mark Tansey referred to, borrowing from philosophy but really retooling the term as metaphoric re-description, with the idea that we're not actually making explicit, nor in a sense negating the importance of the work, we're supplying a supplementary fantasy. And this is a way of reading the artist critic/relationship. You know Greenberg's artist/critic relationship, with Danto's dependence on the Brillo box, Beuys's dependence on Kabakov as a kind of supplemental fantasy act whose real home is in poetics. And this sort of interested me because we say to ourselves, "well, the facts can be known, but the ordering of the facts can't be known—it can only be written." And then we follow this line of logic to the idea that we're more consumed with critiquing projects. It seems to me that one of the dirty rumors of project-oriented art is that art has become too much like students. But I'm interested in the notion that critics would form a sort of parasitic poetic supplementary relationship with students themselves, or with the notion of the student audience, because it's a consequential audience, and it's a consuming audience.

Kristina Lee Podesva: Recently *Fillip* hosted Julian Myers from CCA [California College of the Arts] in San Francisco. He gave a talk for a catalogue essay he's writing for *Vitamin 3D* about sculptural practices, and in particular he looked at three Los Angeles artists. One of the things that he touched on at the end of his talk was this pedagogical problem, and the pedagogical problem for him is that it seems, more recently—and this was probably true during the days of the Salon and the Academy—that artists, when they come out of MFA programs, are rewarded when they reproduce the discourses of their art-star teachers. So I'm not sure if I'm exactly answering what

you are trying to say, but I thought that was quite interesting in terms of the reproduction of discourse, how it functions both in the review form but also this pedagogical problem through the students, through a kind of genealogy certain art stars feel they are "owed" in a sense. So it's a very real problem. I definitely think that instructors and professors of art, particularly those who are quite famous, do teach their students about strategies, about certain kind of styles, about certain kinds of key words that they should then reproduce in order to get the shows, the gallerists, etc. But I don't think that's necessarily a new problem—just new in the last forty years, not before then.

William Wood: With regard to that, I think of Howard Singerman's book on the history of the MFA [*Art Subjects: Making Artists in the American University*], where he makes it clear that the reason people go for graduate studies in art practice is that artists teach artists. Teachers teach students in grade school, in BFA programs artists teach students, then in MFA programs you learn how to be an artist by following those protocols, by learning exactly those protocols. And what I think is interesting—this is a point that is very much stressed in the rest of the discussions in this seminar and the *State of Art Criticism* book that James Elkins and Michael Newman put together—is that they're saying criticism can't be taught, or it hasn't been taught. I mean, there are courses you can take on the history of criticism within art history departments, but rarely do you get someone who can teach this. So they say, "Well, what would you do?" So maybe it doesn't have that corpus attached to it, or that ability to be slotted into, as Singerman proves how the MFA programs had to be slotted into the research and disciplinarity of the university in order to be accepted there. That criticism might not be able to do that for a number of reasons—some of that heteronomy of the relationship of writing to money—is something that is problematic to try to teach.

Tom Morton: I should probably point out that one of our speakers this afternoon actually teaches an MFA course in critical art writing. And, I wonder, is there a professional aspect to that, Maria? Do you teach them about getting writing gigs?

Maria Fusco: I should say a couple of things about the [art writing MFA] program at Goldsmiths, but I don't want to talk too much, because I have my time this afternoon. It's a new program, so we don't really have a clue what we're doing with it, which is brilliant and also terrible at the same time. My comment earlier was that Michael Newman is one of my colleagues at Goldsmiths, and he actually teaches the history of criticism and how to write it. So I was commenting on the irony of the last comment about Elkins. Something I was thinking about when we were talking about canonical duplication through students—and I was thinking about this earlier in regards to writing reviews—is that maybe it is easier to duplicate the things that are easy, and that's how canons perhaps are built, upon easiness and simplicity (rather in the way […] books, which are successful in that you get the soufflé at the end, often sell better). So I wonder if the stratification of simplification and duplication are all very closely aligned with each other, and if that's why you get

this replication—because the things that are easier to do are the things that get picked up. And it might be more to do with that rather than being told to replicate—it might be that the people who replicate do so because they pick the easiest points to copy.

Kristina Lee Podesva: Well, it's also, I think, legitimated by critics who say, "I've seen that before. I recognize that." And it's much easier to, as you say, reproduce that sort of that commentary.

Maria Fusco: Sina Najafi from *Cabinet* magazine said something which I think is a very interesting comment and really [speaks] to this idea of distributive writing practices. He talked about how when they began *Cabinet* the only idea they had was that they wanted to write their readers into existence. Apart from that, they didn't really have a particular idea [about the magazine]. And this idea of contingency, which I think I'll touch on this afternoon so I'll try not to talk about, is very important, and its really acanonical because you really don't have a clue what you're going for, you just kind of know that you want it, to a certain extent.

Dick Averns: Questions to whomever, but it was prompted by Bill mentioning relational aesthetics. I'm intrigued to hear how people might interpret the role of that in relation to Boris Groys, who's obviously come up a lot, and his opening essay in *Art Power* (if I recall correctly it is called the "The Logic of Equal Aesthetic Rights"). To make a generalization—and it might be good that I make a generalization so people on the panel can more clearly define this kind of material for the broader audience—[the book] seems to distinguish between art that falls within the realm of the market and operates through the financial currency, which we've heard about, and then maybe autonomous art objects that are outside of that. So if I can make that kind of generalization or summation of his logic of equal aesthetic rights, how does something like relational aesthetics fit within that framework? I also want to footnote it by hearing some views perhaps on the legitimacy of Nicolas Bourriaud's claim that relational aesthetics isn't a corollary to earlier movements, as he attempts to make it. It seems to want to be something new, which of course people are always wanting to be, but it does seem that origins around Fluxus, conceptual art practices, Happenings, the evolution of video practices, and so forth are all important forerunners to give this legitimization to relational aesthetics. So how does relational aesthetics fit in with all that? It's possibly a project, as Bill might say, but how do we go with this?

William Wood: I raised *Relational Aesthetics* in terms of its fantasy of reconnection and of immediacy and so on. I would probably describe Bourriaud's work as Lütticken did, as "a pathetic tangle of slogans and hype." Bourriaud would be the type of critic that Lütticken would be taking aim at in saying, "you're bringing in a whole pile of cultural theory irresponsibly and trying to apply it." I mean, [the idea that relational aesthetics is somehow outside of a market is absolutely absurd. It's basing itself on the idea that it looks like it's not marketable, and then it's immediately marketable. There's always some sort of souvenir attached to it.

Tom Morton: I think I'm probably a bit more sympathetic towards Nicolas's position than you.

William Wood: I'm not saying that I'm not necessarily interested in some of the projects and practices that are lumped under that. It's the labeling and the self-promotional aspect of Bourriaud's work.

Tom Morton: I think it's worth remembering that *Relational Aesthetics* is a series of essays that appeared at different times and was squeezed together into a book. It's worth remembering that the way its been attacked by various people, including Claire [Bishop] most prominently in *October*, hasn't really taken that into account. The sort of patched-togetherness of *Relational Aesthetics* as a project, and Nicolas's involvement with a particular generation of artists, and the claim for it being something new, is more about time and place than some kind of particular formal innovation. It's also worth pointing out how interesting it is that in the absence of other terms as bandied-about as relational aesthetics, this is the one that one comes back to, even though this book was written in, like, 1996. There's a new book by Bourriaud coming out this year. I'd be interested to see if that has the same affect as *Altermodern*. So I think it's worth actually looking at the roots of these things. It's rather been taken like something like Impressionism, you know? It's become a kind of word like that, and it's been rerouted for different purposes by different people.

William Wood: No, I do think that's interesting. I think that might be symptomatic of something that we might not be able to talk about.

As you say, you know we talk about audiences, we talk about creating audiences, we talk about addressing them, we talk about carrying them, and so on, but yet we know how often irresponsibly we act in taking up slogans, in taking up…that sort of stuff such as "*frieze* is so *frieze*." Maybe this is more how to look at it in terms of a field. Holland Cotter insists upon this in the *New York Times* piece that I was citing, where he says that the critics, the curators, the dealers sit down, meet together, spend time together, talk together; no wonder it is a close coterie. In a Bourdieuian sense, it makes perfect sense. Who else is going to read critics except critics, first of all? You want to know what the competition is doing so you can scoop them. You want to be able to create your usually subtle and indirect attack upon them by treaty with another artist—or maybe it's overt, such as Claire Bishop, which is quite strong.

Tom Morton: I think that there's something about that project as well, which was, "I want to eat at that *October* table, so Nicolas Bourriaud is the guy I'm going for."

William Wood: I can see that. I guess I'm trying to describe this idea that—thinking about Bourdieu again (especially the lectures he did on television and about journalism)—there is a closed world of interest, or at least a world of influence and involvement between players in the field, that is kind of axiomatic. It's not, like you point out, as if everyone is acting venally; they're acting in their interests, and with their own strategies that have to be operated within that field.

Chris Gergley: I'll try to address as many of the speakers as possible. Many of you cited Boris Groys, and I had the feeling that those of you who did were trying to wiggle around what he might be saying, in that the choice to draw attention to an artist or not, to write about them or not, is a kind of judgment. It's a powerful and authoritative judgment.

That's kind of all we need to constitute a certain knowledge about what's going on in the art world. It might make us uncomfortable, because we might be saying that we have critics and we have curators, [but] we just don't need their texts to know about the artists. All we need to know is who wrote about who and that someone got written up in *frieze*, someone got written about in *Fillip*, an artist wrote something in *Fillip* or they have a project in *Fillip*, is Greenberg in fashion or out of fashion? And that is real knowledge that we can operate with, and it might make us uncomfortable, but I don't think it constitutes a crisis, because I think a crisis would require not having sure footing. In a way, [within] that framework, we do know whom to trust, so it's not a true crisis in the sense that there's not a competing paradigm to offer another model of trust. And so, is it just the lack of texts and their necessity, rather than no critics or writers?

Tom Morton: I'm rather skeptical about the notion of crisis in criticism myself, as I kind of laid out. This idea of selecting is kind of interesting. One of the put-downs that one gets from certain people in London if you work for *frieze* is "I only read *frieze* for the ads," as though going through the ads somehow confirms a kind of judgment. Whether these are ads for arts institutions or commercial galleries, you read the ads and see who is doing well, and this perhaps tells you something. I wouldn't necessarily agree that it's the most useful way to read that or any other kind of publication, but it's a way, I guess. In terms of a selection, what this rather misses out on the idea of there not being text. I mean, certainly a curator's work is not just choosing an artist, it's also working with an artist to realize a show. And there are kind of different degrees of involvement one has, depending on the artist and depending on oneself. So I think that's not so much selecting someone in the way one selects the winner of an art prize. And I'd say, it's usually the decision of curators (whether in an artist-run space or an institution), and on the other hand it's a decision of commercial gallerists that leads critics to write. And that's not just in reviews. Most magazines will make some aim at topicality, and that topicality's basis is on the appearance of artists x and Biennale Y or group show Z. That kind of confirmation has already happened before the kind that critics that draw attention to…if you pay any attention to what is going on. I mean, that's why something like *e-flux* has transformed judgment and reputation enormously. Anyone who signs up for this gets ten or so e-mails a day, and you often don't even need to open them. Often they are very interesting on the subject line; you can get some idea of which artists are doing well, which curators are accruing more power, you know?

Chris Gergley: It's real knowledge about those artists, too…and the judgment is real. Is that what makes us uncomfortable: what judgment is?

Tom Morton: What's real knowledge about those?

Chris Gergley: At least hierarchical knowledge. We know something, some kind of base knowledge, which is rare enough.

Tom Morton: I mean, there's some kind of empiricism to it: an artist's exhibition, a *kunsthalle* exhibition. And I guess one question is how you understand which of those have value as a kind of interesting way into that. What is interesting about what Groys says is this kind of search engine of it, and this isn't all you want to know. A search engine is useful—you go to it, and you use it to find out more about something.

Chris Gergley: But we want to know who to trust, I think.

Tom Morton: And how do you arrive at who you trust?

Chris Gergley: *artnet*. [laughter]

Kristina Lee Podesva: I don't think any of us believe there is a crisis. I think that there isn't necessarily a lack of text, but there might be difficulty in finding the text. I think that's what's happening today. And I think, as Tom pointed out, the Internet is an interesting place in terms of circulating other texts and other discourses, but the question is: How do you find them? So for me, when you do searches on the Internet, you know Google, you can pay Google or meta-tag in certain ways where you become the top search, but that question of distribution is fundamental for me for thinking about how to find the criticism you seek or how to find the publics you seek. If you don't find it, then you need to make those outlets. So, for instance, one example is Tirdad's project with Bad Jens. It is brilliant, because how many people are reading about feminist issues in Iranian society? You have it online, you can search it, you can seek it out. Or let's just say if you're interested in Tirdad's practice as a writer or as a curator; you can search his name, and then you will also find this particular space for a different kind of writing, a different kind of criticism. I think that's how you then circulate some of these other texts. Some people lament the fact that there aren't enough texts. I think there are plenty of texts; it's just a matter of finding them.

Chris Gergley: Yeah, one last comment. It's not pure buzz, though. I think that it's still sophisticated enough that we can piece together who's talking about who, and who's showing who…. It's real in some sense, not just hits on Google. That would be a kind of cynical view, but I think it's still sophisticated in its own system, and it seems to operate well.

Mohammad Salemy: I wanted to go back to what Tirdad was talking about yesterday—that there is no crisis in criticism. But I think the crisis is more like the modes of judgment, and, to simplify it, the crisis of bad judgment. Immediately you're saying, okay, what is good, what is bad? It's more like inconsequential judgment. And to give you a couple of examples: MoMA's first show, which opened very close to the 1929 crash, was Alfred Barr's first curated show (because the first show was actually a post-Impressionist Van Gogh show). It was called *19 American Painters of Now*, or something like that, and only a couple of those people are known or recognized,

and the seventeen others, we don't even know who they are. Actually there is so little on the show on the Internet; I've been searching for a month, and I can't get the list of the nineteen people, because MoMA doesn't want to acknowledge that show, even though it was an important show, [and] it was the first curated show at MoMA.

John O'Brian: That's not true. It's all in the archives.

Mohammad Salemy: But it's not accessible on the Internet. I can't even get the name of the nineteen people.

John O'Brian: If it's not on the Internet, it doesn't mean it doesn't exist.

Mohammad Salemy: I'm not saying it doesn't exist, but still it's sort of like an inconsequentiality of the people who were in that show when we look back. And now, because you disagree with me, I almost forgot my contemporary example. But basically, going back to the mode of judgment—there are a lot of judgments that are all around us, but they're just expressed in a different way. But mostly the problem is the mode of judgment; it's sort of like the superficiality of the judgment, actually, that's being passed on beyond all these complicated concepts and words. My closest comparison to art criticism today is fashion criticism and the way fashion is written about in fashion magazines, but particularly around New York fashion week, when they throw those shows two seasons before, and the writers write about that. It's very similar, but the fashion writers are honest about how superficial it is—name-dropping and all that stuff that Tom was talking about. It's sort of like:

How consequential is the judgment, the judgments that are being made right now about particular artists or particular stuff?

William Wood: I think that in this call for judgment we're forgetting something which John alluded to (and certainly was part of my historical research on conceptual art), [and that] is how boring it was to keep reading Clement Greenberg and Michael Fried saying that Jules Olitski and Frank Stella were the greatest painters of our day when they were seen as totally irrelevant. And how boring it was to keep them and their acolytes judging the same way all the time. And part of what I was trying to get at in my paper was that you have to have a whole set of attitudes not towards what you're saying, but towards what the object of your study is. A whole set of preconceptions and perhaps narrow views in order to maintain that idea of "we know where you stand, we can judge you." So to make your judgment consequential might be to actually…. And here again, I think I'm borrowing from ideas that Charles Harrison says, which is that, you know, it inevitably misrepresents the object.

Mohammad Salemy: Maybe I didn't use the right word, but what I meant by consequential is historically consequential. And I remembered my example. I don't know if you know this or not but I recently found out that Jack Shadbolt used to write some art criticism. And actually, he saw the first drip paintings of Jackson Pollock, and he hated them. When he came back to Vancouver he wrote about them and he completely dissed the show, and he said "they look like newspapers from under the bird cage."

William Wood: And that wasn't on the Internet, was it, Mo?

Tom Morton: "What would consequential criticism look like?" would be my question. There is some really stupid art writing out there. One of my guilty pleasures, that maybe many of you share, is *Artforum*'s Scene and Herd page and *Vice Magazine*'s Do's and Don'ts—they teach me more about judgment and criticism now than any amount of Boris Groys. To some degree, the historically consequential, that will work itself out in time, you know? And there's a conversation that we have, maybe about criticism and the idea that it was always the first draft of art history and whether that's even possible at a time such as ours where there is so much information, so many artists, a proliferation of communication technology….

William Wood: But that might also relate to the question that Chris Gergley was raising about identification of critics with certain artists, right? That idea of whether it's Fried and Stella, or Buchloh and Lawrence Weiner, who do you trust? You trust the person who has actually stuck it out, and the person who has actually paid attention and followed a career and worked almost in collaboration. Again, Buchloh with Michael Asher, working in collaboration with him on the documentation of his work. So that says, I'm sticking with this person. And presumably—and one hopes this would be the problem—if it simply repeats or spreads only just insider information…or does it actually deepen over time? That would be the question, about whether that commitment does or doesn't. I would also think about what Chris was thinking about, too, in remembering

Willy Bongard's statistical analysis and capital from the late sixties on that would rank the top one hundred artists in this German business magazine. He would use shows, auction prices, critical mentions, the type of institution they were in—it was a pretty sophisticated analysis. It could be more sophisticated now, but maybe we should think about reviving it now. Is it still going?

Diedrich Diederichsen: It's still going.

Mohammad Salemy: I just want to say that the term I used, "historically consequential," has a lot to do with the paradoxical nature of contemporary art, from modernism until now, where the art itself claims to be the art of now but it's always projected in the future. It's art of now, but this is the art that will be understood even better fifty years from now, or one hundred years from now. And like the project of criticism, it's like it's a criticism of the art of now, but it's supposed to be relevant or important years after now as well. Like Buchloh, who presented a paper in Vancouver called "Figures of Authority," right? Which was later on printed in *Artforum* and dealt a big blow to new expressionist painters.

Gabriel Saloman: I wanted to try to pick up some threads that I feel are dangling from earlier and maybe talk a little bit about artists in relationship to art criticism. I'm not sure if anyone in this room has read Jean Genet's *The Balcony*, but there's a really profound scene in that play that takes place in a brothel, and the clients of this brothel role-play as figures of importance in society (judges and army generals, etc.), and the women working often play the role of the working class or the under class, that are sort of subjected to their power structure. And there's a scene where the judge, who is a brothel client, is condemning a thief who is played by a prostitute, and suddenly in the midst of the role-play the thief (the prostitute) refuses to acknowledge that she's a thief, and suddenly she steps away and says "well, what if I didn't steal anything?" The judge goes from being in this position of power to suddenly crawling on his knees, begging at her feet, "please tell me you stole something, you have to have stole something, otherwise I can't be a judge." He's absolutely horrified at the possibility that this role-play won't continue, but then because of the economic circumstances, of course, she reneges and says, "oh, no I am a thief, so that I can continue with the role-play and I can get paid for my work." This is one potential relationship that I see. But I would like to counter that, if I may. My counter is that this may actually relate somewhat to relational aesthetics, but I want to talk more to social practices as an emerging form ([that] has been emerging for decades). I want to suggest that right now that particular practice is reaching a crisis of a lack of judgment and a lack of criticism. I think that within its pure role, there are people that have been doing this work for a while, like Ted Purves, who has actually done some important writing on it, but there is not a very clear system of judgment. Of course, part of this is [that] as a practice they've stepped away from making completely enclosed projects that can be perceived as souvenirs in a marketplace. Instead, it's entered into a metaphysical realm that I think all art alludes to, but its metaphysics are its finished product, where the work is completed by the experience of those who participate, or those who witness, or even those who read about it or think about it. I feel as though it's been used to create a comfort zone for those artists in that project and in that sphere, where they no longer need to be judged because their art is a gift—and how can you judge a gift? But I actually think, as a practitioner, that it's a huge issue, and I disagree, and I'm really frustrated that there is such a lack of judgment and a lack of concern in creating criteria by which to understand the effectiveness, the value, or the validity, of that work. So if you want to speak to that, I'd be very grateful.

Rob Stone: There's a question here about authorship, about becoming a writer in the framework of being an object in relationship to art practices. So you become interested in art works, certainly—the contexts of their production, certainly—but all sorts of things about dandruff and other things creep into your life that might form a set of relationships that are both a subject and a subjec-tive relationship, and art criticism is shifting more in that direction. So if there is a criticism in art, a crisis in art criticism, and if there is a crisis that needs to be sustained and dwelled upon, it's of that kind of order, where the things that you bring into relationship with each other reflect back on the morpholo-gies that you are used to using and render them useless so you have to invent new ones. You might have to lie about the things you're talking about, you might have to invent narrators who you can't rely on or depend upon, you might have to do all sorts of things, but yet to do that you have to become a writer, and

you can't just turn out the hundred-and-fifty-pounds an article pieces to get around that problem. There's something more political at stake in that.

February 28, 2009
Panel Two
Panelists: Diedrich Diederichsen
and Maria Fusco
Moderator: Jeff Derksen

Jeff Derksen: Both [of today's] panels presented us with the role of publics, both monochromatic and emergent—although I think those two merged at one point—and we've been oscillating through a dialectic of inductive and deductive evaluations of the art object. But both [Maria Fusco and Diedrich Diederichsen's] papers cross or cohere perhaps in a notion of temporality. What was most compelling to me in Maria's work was the notion of the critical temporality built through narrative and its breakdown; by embedding the critical apparatus in a character (a fiction) that then loses the boundaries between the art object and the role of the critic. In Diedrich's paper, he presented two positions: the critique of bourgeois eternity—which we all do over our morning coffee—and the critique of the possibility of the moment of utopia, which dialectically spun out of [...] by giving us other temporal options to rethink the art object and objecthood itself. Provocatively, at the end, he returned to an understanding of progress as having the potential to critique regression. This seemed to lie parallel to developmental notions of capital, which are ideas that have been tossed out as being, themselves, regressive. We have to return to a progressive sense of regression in order to critique regression, and to therefore have a temporal grasp of the present moment as being unevenly distributed (in terms of its senses but also in terms of the material and wealth that is generated by it), which then also frames one's relation to the art object. So I think the relationship between the art object and temporality in both papers is what ultimately gets troubled. So with that brief synthesis we will open the field for questions.

Rob Stone: To come up with new kinds of art objects and to talk about the relationships that might exist between them, there has to be a kind of uncomfortable autobiography involved.... And I was wondering, talking about the idea of a misplaced Marxism and a phallus that maybe doesn't work, I was wondering how you kind of articulate those as autobiographical materials in the way you were talking.

Maria Fusco: Is that for me? [laughter] I'm very interested in transubstantiation. For those who weren't brought up Catholic, transubstantiation is kind of like a mega-metaphor—the moment in Catholicism when the host is changed from being the host to becoming the body and blood of Christ. It still looks like a wee piece of wafer, but it is the body and blood of Christ, and it's a mysterious, magical, spiritual moment. And I'm very interested—and have always been, having been brought up Catholic in Ireland—in how it can be the wee wafer and be the body and blood of Christ at the same time. And to me, that kind of autobiographical material, if you like—and that piece that I read, that's quite an unusual piece for me in some ways—it's always the same material, in a way. So it's not a reductive viewing of the material in an effort to transform the material. The material has qualities of transformation about it, depending on which bit you look at.

Diedrich Diederichsen: I would say that you can't have an aesthetic experience that you cannot share. I mean, of course, you can never share the aesthetic experience because, by its definition, it's a subjective experience.... You experience everything by yourself, in real time. But this is experience and not aesthetic experience.

Jeff Dersken: The developmental theories of capital are seen as too teleological and should be shied away from. And therefore the notion of progress, of development, has been shied away from and has been off the table. In the way that you put it, we have to return to a sense of progress in order to be able to critique when there is regression. Whereas it seems to me that the power play that happened within neoliberalism was to both hold on to a notion of progress yet freeze it in the present, a continuous present.

Diedrich Diederichsen: But the idea of neoliberalism is now that socialism is gone, everything is possible and that's why nothing is possible. That's the logic, and so there is no history.

Jeff Derksen: So now that socialism is gone, everything is possible, yet all that's left is liberal democracy. So please enjoy it in the present.

Diedrich Diederichsen: So nothing is possible. There's no future.

Jeff Derksen: Right. There's absolutely no future. There's just this brilliant utopian present of liberal democracy in neoliberalism.

Diedrich Diederichsen: Yes, but the fact is that just because there's an ideology [that there is] no history, doesn't mean that...as we can see right now. And I think it's interesting, if you look at a lot of cultural products that are out right now, like the film *Revolutionary Road* or the TV series *Mad Men*, they are all about, in a kind of clumsy way, trying to reintroduce the idea of progress by showing us how far we got, showing the worst forms of sexism and racism not so long ago [in a way that suggests]: "look what we've achieved since then!" And this is, of course, a highly sentimentalist idea of progress. But it somewhat reflects the necessity to re-describe that history has certain possibilities, and it's not just contingent.

Jeff Derksen: Which was actually the brilliance of George Bush's philosophy of history, which was that we're in this beautiful neoliberal present, the war has been won, the market will always sustain itself, but then as soon as that utopian moment of neoliberalism cracked, so did the use of history. Then it was: "History will be the judge." So the notion of history is exactly invoked again. Once they had stalled it—like a huge pause button had been put on the notion of history to hold it in a continuous present—then the minute it became viable to refigure themselves, progress continues.

Alissa Firth-Eagland: I just want to come back to this link, Jeff, you were making in the beginning. Or maybe it wasn't a link, but I see a bit of a link. You were talking about interdisciplinary, specifically methodological possibilities. Then you went on to speak about the poetics of critical engagement, and it seems to me that there's a link between these two things. Especially when I think of what Kristina [Lee Podesva] was saying earlier, when she quoted Sven Lütticken. I'm really glad that "the critical forms of publicness" was brought into this discussion, because it's something that I'm really interested in. So, I guess I have a naïve, formal question, but would anyone on the panel like to talk about a link between interdisciplinary and the poetics of critical engagement?

Jeff Derksen: Maybe I'll rather unfairly shift it over to Maria, because I think that's actually what was happening in the second part of your paper [presented, in excerpt, in the current volume as footnotes to Fusco's essay –Eds.]. I don't want to make such a big genre split between the two, but it was interdisciplinarity or transdisciplinarity that produced a poetics of critical engagement, let's say. And also it suggested a narrative time that broke the normative relationship of the temporality of the object. So, by moving narrative structures into the discipline of art writing or criticism, you make a different poetics. I'm using poetics as a productive aspect of a text. Does that make sense?

Maria Fusco: Yes, thank you, that does. Does that answer your question? [laughs]

Alissa Firth-Eagland: It does, but I think it's worth saying that—or maybe it's fairly obvious—there's certainly a temporal shift that occurred now in the audience when you delivered [that portion of your] text. And that was a very specific example of an interdisciplinary approach, and I guess I'm just really thankful to have had that.

Maria Fusco: Well, thank you.

My colleague at Goldsmiths, Adrian Rifkin, doesn't believe in something being interdisciplinary, because he thinks that it's a product of process rather than a part of a procedure, and I think I might sort of agree with that. I'll have that on one hand and then on the other hand I'll say the Yogi Berra quote: "You can see a lot by looking." [*sic*: "You can observe a lot just by watching" –Eds.] And that maybe what's important is how closely you are looking, and perhaps not where you're looking from. I don't make differentiations between different ways of working, however, clearly I'm aware that they exist. And I'm also aware that particular pieces of work can live in different places, depending on where I choose to put them or I'm invited to put them. So interdisciplinarity to me doesn't seem to.... I really don't think about it. Clearly I'm cognizant and aware, but it's not something that ever particularly occurs to me. Another example of that might be my program with Goldsmiths, the writing program. Most of the people in the program call themselves artists. We only have one person who calls himself a writer.... When starting a new program [we] thought "oh, wouldn't it be great. It'll be full of people who call themselves art writers." But they call themselves artists, so in a sense it was kind of a return to the nomenclature of a discipline rather than a desire to re-name it. And that's actually being very productive because it recalibrates the possibilities for the work that is produced within it, because it's going back to a kind of starting point of a department, if you like, and a kind of name of practice rather than trying to make up a new name. And I should just add that I think art writing is a really dreadful term. I haven't thought of a better one just yet—maybe in the future.

David Khang: Perhaps a dismantling of criticality in the visual art world becomes a productive space. And I could see that happening [in the second half of Maria's paper], and I would concur with the validity of that phenomenon, but there's also an overlapping phenomenon that is happening that David Josselit points out. That is the dismantling of critical function that goes beyond the art community. I see that happening in the scientific community as well. So in our own midst is—and this is where Tirdad's triple "criticism, critique, and criticality" comes in—a commercial gallery assistant's commentary that said "our artists' works are inflected with criticality without being critical." So I see the three— the criticism, critique, and criticality—and if they are resting against one another, and dependent on one another to work interdependently, how do you have one without the other two, and what do you do in a cultural field where one can, through words, arguably, escape and then create an unproductive space?

Jeff Derksen: I'd just like to make a brief comment and then open the discussion up. I was pointing towards the movement where one shifts between sites and fields—and let's say different methodologies— and finds a greater freedom in one than the other. This is, in a sense, a movement from one set of determinations to another. Perhaps naïvely, not recognizing the new set of determinants, this can be exuberant in some way—whether it's 750 words and the quick publication [of a review assignment] versus the endlessness of academic writing. I don't see this shifting between two sites

as a loss of criticality, but, hopefully, I would think of this as a movement that would produce new forms of critique. If I remember correctly from last night, Tirdad used the final aspect within that triad of criticalities [as a] kind of a turn inward, a turn away from the social. And my point in the introduction was that when we turn away from the social it signals a crisis within the field. So, I think that, in some ways, what we've been talking about today is the production of the crisis in art writing, and what would be the relationship between that generated crisis, and—to use an old term—the "actual existing" crisis out in the social field. That, to me, is the fascinating question at the moment. If there is a crisis in art writing, it is the inability to move between this crisis of cultural and the crisis of the social. So the movement from the cultural field to the social field, which John O'Brian was actually doing very nicely in his comments today, is key. Rather than a loss of criticality as you move between different disciplines, I was thinking of the kind of critical methodological shifting that Diedrich's work is an exemplar of, which I see as an opening of possibilities as you move through different discourses and methodologies. For instance, the way today that a notion of reception—to blur these two poles—is also being productive…to invoke that older and problematic cultural studies notion of productive consumption. Maybe those two poles of production and reception, in a sense, in the paper that you gave today was the source of the dialectic and not a rejection of closure (which I think is synonymous with [the notion of] judgment we've been using today). So "the poetics of a rejection of closure" becomes a strong dialectical point. I think the compelling term you used was "overwhelment."

Diedrich Diederichsen: My point is basically that judgment restores a relation between the recipient to herself or himself, making it possible to continue not to close. So the closure of judgment—the final decision—enables one to continue. Postponing judgment only makes things slowly fade away and die out. It is something that is basically lived; it's visibly and articulately lived in music oriented communities. It is also lived in the same art communities that we are living in…. We leave this room and talk about the last show we've seen. Every art conversation I had in the last two or three days went, "Did you like that show?" or "Did you like that show better than this one?" Of course, this is not only an empty thing. These conversations are full of reasons that are given by both sides which are continuously enabling us to go on. The fact that this aspect of our daily art conversation is so absent from criticism is a clear indication of what you could call ideology or orthodoxy. There is obviously, in the world, a certain practice and a certain consciousness active, widespread, visible, observable, and not represented in the cultural production of the same. That is, I think, the clearest case of ideology.

Tirdad Zolghadr: I just wanted to respond to [David Khang's] question. I also have to add that this three-step that I introduced yesterday of criticism, critique, and criticality was coined by Irit Rogoff, and it tries to grapple with the possibility of distance which is implicit, at least in the most conventional sense of the term. And usually the question is not the way you phrased it. You said,

"How can you have criticality without the other two?" And the way it was framed—for example, today, the last panel—was more something along the lines of (at least the way Diedrich framed it) "How can you have it along with…how can you have criticality *and* the other two together?" And if I understood correctly, it's a form of strategic essentialism, the way Diedrich is positing the moment of judgment as a necessary moment of closure—an appropriation of something which is artificial to begin with, perhaps?

Diedrich Diederichsen: I often sympathize with the idea of strategic essentialism in several constellations, because in strategic essentialism you are holding something up that you clearly do not believe in for strategic reasons. The strategic reasons, of course, have a certain reality so you believe in that reality that makes it necessary, but you don't believe it as a cognitive object. Whereas with judgment, [the reasons are not] strategic, but because you want a continuation of the process. But it's preliminary—so you believe in it for the moment, but you know it's only for the moment.

Clint Burnham: First of all, always totalize. [laughter] Secondly, yesterday, I think, Tirdad, you were talking about "binary, digital, dialectical fluffing." But maybe I'm thinking of Dr. Dre or something. So you were thinking about pillows, but it got me thinking about porn fluffing. So then I thought, I want more of that, but then, of course, Maria, that's what you did in your story—you brought in the libidinal in a very timely way. But two more critical, or critically oriented, things: I actually want more theory and philosophy and politics in art writing. I know you are not saying that we shouldn't have that, but in my mind, it's one of the few public places where that actually takes place—even within the imagined community or the "publics and counterpublics" (in Michael Warner's terms). But two final things: The discussion today about intimacy and the one yesterday about proxemics and space and distance, and so on. I was thinking about those kind of things, in part because of Andrea Fraser's notion of self-reflexivity. I think it's an example of [Slavoj] Zizek's fetishistic disavowal. Which is to say: "I know very well, and I'm complicit in the institution, but by going through this [and so forth]...." For me [Pierre] Bourdieu is the name that is very important to keep in this conversation in the way William Wood directed it earlier today. I think that self-reflexive moment of the critic becomes a way to continue on doing business as usual—to contribute to that sort of flow. Finally, my main point, and maybe this will come back to what the panel wants to talk about: I think that there's a kind of anxiety about judgment. Just to bring it back into the local in terms of local politics here—the government announced yesterday that they want a minimum sentencing requirement for drug dealers of different kinds. There's a gang war going on. One year for marijuana dealers, two for coke dealers, and so on and so forth. Which is the fantasy that the judge is not strict enough. We have prisons that are overcrowded, but the judges aren't strict enough. Which translates, I think, into the question: "are the critics strict enough?" Are they letting things slide because of a postmodern morass where "there are no standards"?

Maria Fusco: Within your observation about the strictness of critics and their relationship with the judge, there's a presupposition there that the critic has power. I know that it's popped up over the last couple of days, and I'm not sure about it. I wonder if it's that the objects themselves aren't strict enough, rather than the critics, perhaps. As you know, objects such as the deodand had a legal liability, and objects could be hung, as well as the person who had used the object to kill someone. So yes, I wonder maybe if the objects need to be stricter, and I wonder if the objects ultimately have more power than the critics have, really. There's that kind of lack of judgment and possibly a lack of strictness, as you put it. Maybe this is a correct method to proceed [with] in order to establish a methodology of art writing. And, in a way, the method seems quite clear, but the overarching methodology seems to be the problem or the problematic, depending on how you look at it.

Diedrich Diederichsen: But then also judgment in terms of judges and law, and judgment in terms of art, are two opposed practices—they are the opposite of each other. So if someone has either a sadistic or masochistic fantasy of what judges should do in the real world and projecting that on what critics should do in the art world, that would be clearly a misunderstanding, I think.

Maria Fusco: There's an excellent essay by a woman named Jane Bennett who's a political theorist. The essay is called *Thing Power*. It's fantastic. And she says that you need to exercise extreme caution with things that could damage you.

Jordan Strom: My question is sort of a personal one I guess, or a selfish one, going back to narcissism. I wanted to ask you a question about the review form. This is a question more for you, Maria—however both of you may have a response. One thing that T. J. Clark elegantly put together in his book *The Sight of Death* is about art writing and how art writing is meant to sort of write the work of art to death. We've circled back to the idea of the review. Tirdad was saying reviews tend to be about as self-reflective as an Italian opera. I was quite buoyed by [Tom Morton's suggestion that] the review is sort of the heart of *frieze* magazine. I was at a conference in Rotterdam where so many of the magazine editors were talking about reviews as more of a kind of breeding ground for emerging writers, like just kind of a training, a place were maybe the most advanced writing wasn't taking place. One of the things with *Fillip* we were trying to consider was trying to re-vivify or re-enliven review writing, giving more space to the review, as Kristina talked about. At the time, in 2004, when we started thinking about the magazine, we were interested in bringing the art writing closer together with art criticism, this sort of freeway that tends to run through them, between them. Trying to make that into kind of an ever-flowing stream. How can they exist, how can they come together to an extent, how can we kind of reinvigorate the review form? I was curious if you had some examples within the *Happy Hypocrite*—the first couple issues you've edited—where you could identify a certain piece of writing that operates as a kind of exhibition or event review combined with a type of innovative fictional or non-fictional mode of writing?

Maria Fusco: I don't know if I can identify it exactly in the *Happy Hypocrite* because I don't think that is what the *Happy Hypocrite's* role is. The *Happy Hypocrite* was devised as a space that was ontologically opposed to the review, not because I'm opposed to the review but just because I wanted to create a forum for different types of writing. Actually there are a lot of forums for reviews, whether small or large. I'm very keen on reviews. I think reviews are more interesting and accomplished and arguably have a higher level of engagement than a feature piece or a catalogue essay. In terms of the first issue of the *Happy Hypocrite*, I would flag up Jared Burns. Jared Burns—well they [his reviews] are poems, really, footnoted poems. He's obsessed with the Loch Ness Monster as an ur example of representation. And, possibly, if I had it here, I would read it out a bit, but I won't say much more than that, because in terms of how one might approach an idea of representation and how one might use inscriptive rather than descriptive purposes, in my view, descriptive writing is necessary in a review context, especially if someone isn't getting to see something. You have to give some idea of what it looks like, after all. But I would be very opposed to something that was just descriptive rather than inscriptive. A personal example might be in the scent of an answer rather than a response. I wrote a review—it must be about three or four months ago, now—for a British publication called *Art Monthly*. It was a review of Steve McQueen's *Hunger*. Have you seen *Hunger* yet? Well, *Hunger*, I'm sure most of you know, is a ninety-minute feature film that's based in a prison in Northern Ireland during the time of the hunger strikers. And because of my personal experience, I felt compelled to write about it but was also very worried about the kind of leakage of subjectivity over the top of it. So at the beginning of the review I sort of stated my position, that it was a bit ridiculous me writing about it. I was far too close to the subject matter. So generally [the review] was very positive. But in the end I found a major problematic with the film, which was that I felt that it wasn't about politics—which I felt it should have been—and I went into details that I won't bore you with now. And in the following issue of *Art Monthly*, Steve McQueen wrote a letter which was sent through his gallery, not him directly, which I thought was quite interesting (of course he's entitled to reply to it). But he said in the letter—and I am paraphrasing, obviously—he said that the research he had done for the film proved that the point I had made in the review was incorrect because it was his research and he'd done it. To which I thought the whole point of doing a review is that one might have one's own personal research: that I grew up in a Catholic ghetto when it was all going on, living with, being neighbours with the people who were in the prison. I tried to address this as a kind of mode of art writing in a review con-text, and to have a response which returned to the priority of research as objectivity was hilarious and also really irritating. I was really pissed off. But I felt that I shouldn't be. I was encouraged to respond to his letter, but I felt that I was pointless because I thought that I had done the work that I had needed to do in the review, and to do any more work would just be redundant. I don't know if that ap-proaches your question, but I think it's the closest I can get.

Holly Ward: Isn't that an example also of the point you just made, about the rigour of the object?

Maria Fusco: What do you mean by that?

Holly Ward: [McQueen's argument is that if] you've done research then you're speaking as an authority—that compounded by being the maker of the piece. You've got an argument that talks about a kind of rigor. It is, I believe, Diedrich's point, that it is very difficult to take a critical stance when you are standing against the social field in which you operate.

Diedrich Diederichsen: Critical reviews are such a rarity in the art world that it increases their value, like all rare things are valuable. But, on the other hand, it makes them even more dramatic. I think one can do a study that fifty percent of all critical reviews in all art maga-zines of the last twelve months have caused replies (because they are so rare). Sometimes the replies were printed, sometimes the replies were sent to the editor. [In this one case] an artist wrote in: "Two years ago I gave an edition to this magazine and now you are writing badly of me. What kind of assholes are you?" Or something like that. [laughter] "And of course, you will never get an edition from me or the gallery that's representing me." It's so rare, and I think something can be done about this. If you look, for example, at a discipline like theater, ballet, dance, critical reviews are more widespread and the reactions are, also. Well, people are pissed, but people deal with it in a different way. People are not sworn enemies afterwards, which is much more healthy and makes other aspects of theatre discourse—which is very old fashioned in other aspects—really very lively.

Mohammad Salemy: One little note: Maria quoted someone as saying, "Don't say yes, say maybe."

Jeff Derksen: It was the title of an essay of hers that I referred to.

Mohammad Salemy: This is like shopping advice, right? Like when you go to shop for clothing, they say, if you wear it in front of the mirror, if it's a yes it's a maybe, if it's a maybe it's a no, if it's a no get out of there. The other point [I want to raise] is how criticism and art writing affects the actual practice of art-making by contemporary artists. If you look around, more than a third of the room [is] filled with practicing artists. Artists read these pieces of text more in depth, unlike anybody else, to the last word. How does that affect, immediately, their practice in the studio?

Maria Fusco: How do you think it affects it?

Mohammad Salemy: I know it affects it. It enters you. Once it enters you, it's right there, and you have to deal with it when you're in the studio making art, right?

Maria Fusco: Just to clarify, are you talking about, more specifically, writing about your work or writing about any work that may concern you?

Mohammad Salemy: Any work—the way contemporary art discourse is written about, and how we as artists read it and then go back to make work, and how that immediately affects the art-making. And on another

point, I just want to say that something that was kind of disappointing in the talks was how everyone on the panels and the keynote speaker talked about the economic crisis as a side dish. Or how just mentioning it is enough to say: "I'm current, I'm contemporary."

Jeff Derksen: I actually had it as a main dish, also with some meat, and it had potatoes and some vegetables.

Mohammad Salemy: It's always assumed that even as deep and dark a crisis this is, it will be dealt with like the Depression, and we're going to be back with some form of new capitalism. But this sick patient may actually die. And I wonder if the fact that we don't want to get deep into it has something to do with the fact that the sickness of this patient has nothing to do with our historic[al] criticality. The death of this patient, or [his] serious sickness, has nothing to do with what we've done, but it has to do with its own structural flaws and its own inherent contradictions. I feel guilty that capitalism is on its deathbed. It may resurrect, but we, as critical people, we, as people who wrote about it, have nothing to do with it. I mean, we all remember when [Jacques] Rancière was [in Vancouver] like a year ago, and his position was like, capitalism is here to stay, and we, the intellectuals, are, at best, ventriloquists. We can be the internal voice of capitalism to itself, kind of guilting it, and pointing it to the little problems here and there, because, basically, capitalism is here to stay.

Maria Fusco: There were three points there, weren't there? Just to paraphrase, the first one had to do with yes, no, and maybe. I would be more inclined to say "maybe" rather than "yes" or "no." The second point had to do with affecting artists' production through writing about it. A quick response, because I'm conscious of time, would be that I'm pathologically polite and wouldn't ever set out to upset anybody but really don't care if I do or not. [laughter] And the third point would have to do with an economic crisis being an entrée or the starter, and how there is this idea of crisis with critical art writing. I don't think that there's a moment of crisis, I don't feel there's a moment of crisis, I don't think it's important enough to be saying there's a moment of crisis, but I like talking about it. [laughter]

Donato Mancini: One thing that I kind of expected to come up at some point, but hasn't, is [the issue] of new forms of pseudo-democratic participation that are proliferating on the Internet, specifically in the form of the judgment of cultural products. This is at the very same time that a lot of critics are thinking about a possible return to judgment. At the same time, judgment in the form of the short review [is proliferating] on different Web sites—you can rate objects from one to five stars. It's not only popular, but it's also becoming cultural common sense, specifically consumerist common sense. I noticed recently the Simon Fraser University library added a star rating system to its library Web site. [laughter] So when you're looking up obscure texts on Mayan linguistics or something, you can give it a star rating. That to me is an indication that all that stuff on the Internet that you see and think of as just noise has actually has become a kind of common sense. How does that bear

on the discussion of judgment and criticism? Secondly, more directly directed at Diedrich: Increasingly consumerism also assumes, or takes the character of, a kind of temporal regime (like you were talking about in music). So [it's] really caught up in a kind of fast-moving temporal regime that, like music, we can't arrest. Would you read these kinds of proliferation of reviews [online] in a similar way to the way you read music reviews?

Diedrich Diederichsen: My slogan for the cultural situation right now is "participation is the new spectacle." What you were describing, the constant encouragement to rate, to have an opinion, to be present, is exactly the same cultural logic that companies expect from their employees these days: an over identification. With recorded music, you only really hear it when you hear it the second time in your life. Not the second time you listen to it but the second time you have a time specific experience with it. The second time [you have] a highly subjective, time-specific experience between yourself and the object that is metonymically connected to it. I think that is an aspect of music temporality— recorded music, of course, only—that you were talking about.

Stan Douglas: I have a couple questions. The first one would relate to a claim that Diedrich has made a couple of times today, that possibly the crisis in criticism today is the fact that the majority of criticism is positive or affirmative—which somehow relates to Maria's suggestion that the problem with a lot of art writing today is not the problem of the writing but of the art that it's talking about. Is that more or less what you said?

Maria Fusco: Yes. [laughter]

Stan Douglas: As an artist, this sounds like a challenge that I have to respond to in some way. [laughter] So I wonder if the crisis in art writing (and frequent experimentation in art writing) appeared simultaneously with the deskilling of artists. As artists became indifferent to craft and less tied to particular disciplines and genres, art writers had to become different kinds of observers: less the traditional art historian and more of a figure who would mimic the artist in some way. So that's one question. The other question is whether art writing could be better if the writer were to take a position. For example, I would always rather be annoyed by reading Theodor Adorno writing about jazz than I would by reading Michael Fried writing about art because they are annoying in different ways. Adorno always asserted a very clear position. He was a very astute listener of music and he believed that the pinnacle of western culture was in the nineteenth century and that it has ever since been in some kind of decline. With that in mind, you can understand his commentary on jazz music, for example. But Michael Fried is always asserting his primacy as the authoritative observer of works of art and how all art fits into his immutable system. I think critics are important, but they are most important or useful to artists when they take a position and don't try and be like us. [laughter]

Diedrich Diederichsen: I couldn't agree more with the second part of what you were saying, especially in relation to Adorno's writing on jazz. I think that those are very useful texts, especially the first one, if you just jumble them around. The invention jazz, as a subject, is absolutely great, I think, but his evaluation of it is completely false. But the way the argument is constructed is very useful, even if he completely misses the subject matter.

Maria Fusco: Well, I've been quite puzzled throughout when it's come up a few times: If you're negative in your writing or are overly critical— negatively critical— you automatically damage your career as a writer. Possibly my writing is incredibly lukewarm [laughter] so it's inoffensive to everybody—that's not something that I've ever considered or come across. I would like to add that there's a lot of bad work about generally; there's a lot of bad writing and there's a lot of bad art, and they're intrinsically linked to one another because they are in the same house at the same time. And I don't see a distinction—I come from a very sort of [Maurice] Blanchot viewpoint—I don't see a distinction between the inside and the outside of the figure. I would find it difficult to understand.... I could pretend I understood (obviously I can, conceptually), but I can't really understand the difference between the inside and the outside of the figure and how, perhaps, the critic behaves in a certain way and the artist behaves in another way. I don't see that differential between them.

Stan Douglas: Do you understand my suggestion that this kind of art writing came at a time when artists were becoming deskilled? Artists were not so concerned with the craft or the technology of picture-making, thing-making, event-making, and so it gives critics the same apparent freedom to do the same thing. As an artist, you are sometimes disappointed by writers because they clearly don't understand what you've done the way the artist might. [laughter] They don't understand the mechanism of picture-making, so you really wish there were competent writers out there who knew the same thing about picture-making, but they are just not there.

Maria Fusco: But why should someone have to understand what you've done?

Stan Douglas: Well, we absolutely have maintain the fantasy that anybody can look at our work and get something out of it. I think that's what any artist has to believe to a certain degree. But when Adorno writes about music, he writes as a musician—he played piano, he studied with [Alban] Berg, and so on. Even though he didn't know what he was talking about, it's still interesting.

Diedrich Diederichsen: Because jazz is a different kind of music than the one he [Adorno] knows—and he actually didn't know anything at all about jazz. But what you're talking about now, this is really what I was referring to earlier. There is [the] production-related knowledge of artists. I don't think it disappeared from critical discourse or writing because writers are deskilled as writers but because in general the focus shifted to other aspects of reception aesthetics. There are, sometimes, specialists, but, in general, people can be very skilled about reception processes and can reproduce and discuss them without knowing anything about how things are made. And just one thing about careers damaged by negative writing: It's a relatively recent phenomenon—the

nineties and this decade—that writers and magazines began having a lot of problems from galleries and artists because of [negative criticism]. Insulting even one person is a much more dangerous bomb then it used to be twenty years ago.

Jeff Derksen: To wrap up, we can come back to Stan's suggestion that writing could be improved if it takes a stand—[an idea that was] actually at the heart of Diedrich's talk today. There can be a use of closure without the fear of closure. Taking a stand is, in some ways, a form of closure, but we have to see that as being productive and not final. And for me, this is where poetics can step in—poetics is a structural aspect that opens.

James Elkins

Afterword

In the last year there were at least five international conferences on art criticism. On the weekend the *Judgment and Contemporary Art Criticism* forum took place, I was at another conference on art criticism in Copenhagen.[1] A few months before, in October 2008, there had been yet another conference on art criticism in Bogotà, Colombia,[2] and in summer 2010 there was a large, four-day conference on the subject in Beijing.[3] Whether or not it makes sense to say that art criticism is in crisis (and I do not believe it does), the field certainly perceives itself as such.

I have been trying to keep up with the literature—something that can't be done for long, at least if you have a day job—and I think that the problems art criticism has been posing to itself are not necessarily endless or insoluble. It helps to distinguish three fundamental philosophic and historical problems, and two underlying rhetorical and institutional reasons why those three problems have not been adequately addressed. I wouldn't claim these are the only five issues that articulate the current conceptualization of art criticism, or even that I'm posing them here in an optimal form, but I do think that until we pay close attention to some version of these issues, art criticism will continue onward in its anxious and inconclusively articulated state.

1. In regard to history

Does art criticism, in its current forms, descend from writers like Charles Baudelaire and Denis Diderot, or are their practices more usefully conceived as parts of other writing traditions? In other words, where does contemporary art criticism begin? In the book *The State of Art Criticism* there is an enormous range of ideas about whether art criticism has a history. For some, like Dave Hickey, art criticism's history comprises whatever creative writers the critic likes. Hickey names William Hazlitt, Thomas de Quincey, Charles Dickens, Oscar Wilde, and others. He names them not because they teach him to write art criticism, because, he says, no one can do that, but because they are his favorite writers. For others, like Steve Melville, art criticism by its very nature doesn't have a history because it depends on the individual act of judging. The range of ideas about whether art criticism has a history is itself much broader than the range of opinion about other central objects of debate in art theory, for example the index in photography, or the place of aesthetics in art history.[4] Art criticism's history, or lack of it, produces a deeper incoherence.

The principal contribution to this problem is Sven Lütticken's essay in this volume, "A Tale of Two Criticisms." He proposes that art criticism has two origins: an Enlightenment tradition, beginning with the French Salon in 1747, and a Romantic tradition, which is "scattered across the early writings of Friedrich Schlegel, Novalis, and others in their circle, around 1800." Several questions could be raised about this genealogy. One might ask how much work these characterizations can do for the present, given that it would not be difficult to demonstrate that Diderot (who is mentioned as an example of an Enlightenment critic) was interested in many things other than "rules" to "regulate the representation of suitable objects in a manner that is morally edifying and ennobling," and that Romantic critiques were not always about "reconstructing" the "shaky rules" established by artworks. In other words, this is a particular reading, done through Jacques Rancière and Walter Benjamin as much as Schlegel or Diderot, which asks to be read not so much for historical veracity as for what work it can do on our practices: and the answer would depend on what lines we can draw between the generations of the late eighteenth and early nineteenth century and the present. My own sense of this is that such lines are tenuous: I would draw them more or less as Michael Newman does in his important essay "The Specificity of Criticism and Its Need for Philosophy" (reprinted in *The State of Art Criticism*) or as Joseph Koerner does in his current (unpublished) work on Breughel. Lütticken argues that our current journalistic criticism often amounts "to a debased Enlightenment criticism that offers judgments without reflection." Leaving aside whether or not Enlightenment critics didn't pause to reflect, the question would be whether we want to assign apparently unreflective moments in contemporary criticism to Enlightenment precursors. If I do, it's because I want to find a deeper history for current art criticism (and then I'd have to ask myself why I want a deeper history); if I don't, it's because I don't see how it helps to see traces of a dissipated Enlightenment in contemporary practices. Is this particular version of the Enlightenment really usefully connected to the present?

2. In regard to the content of art criticism

Should it involve direct judgment, only the consideration of possible judgments, or something more like description of evocation? This was the operative question of the forum, as it has been of others. There is certainly a gulf between the activities of some populist critics, such as Robert Hughes, and certain academic critics, such as Rosalind Krauss. In the two panel discussions held in Ballyvaughan, Ireland, and Chicago, Illinois, transcribed in *The State of*

Art Criticism, I tried posing the problem this way: what kind of conversation might take place between a critic who holds that art criticism's purpose is the articulation of judgment and a critic who sees criticism's purpose as the articulation of the conditions under which critical judgment might be made? I thought putting it this way might avoid a direct interrogation of poststructural interpretations of art criticism, according to which criticism is dedicated to the study of what Krauss called "method"; that is, the elaboration of the assumptions and discursive conditions that lead others to propose judgments. It would also avoid directly questioning those critics who do judge art, either about the reasons they decline to engage with current thinking on the strategies of avoiding judgment, or about more general poststructural concerns. I put the question to Steve Melville and Dave Hickey, and nothing very enlightening took place. Hickey pretended not to see the point of the question, and Melville tentatively articulated an understanding of judgment as a kind of questioning, which would therefore be amenable to the uncertainties that attend or pursue the production of even the most unreflective and apparently immediate judgments. It was a moment, I'd say, of pure darkness. I don't see how anyone reading the transcript of that exchange—between two exemplary practitioners of very different senses of art criticism—could glean any ideas about how art critics might speak to one another across that gulf of judgment.

Diedrich Diederichsen makes an excellent contribution to this debate in his essay for this volume, "Judgment, Objecthood, Temporality." He argues strongly against avoiding judgment, and especially the judgment of value. He has a couple of good arguments to pose against the position he identifies as "the Butler-Foucault-Williams argument," which enjoins a suspension of judgment in favour of an understanding of complexity. For example, he suggests that the production of value judgments creates an ongoing discourse of the kind Judith Butler is said to privilege because "it has to permanently re-discuss what it has seemingly decided for good." He also advances a political critique of the "the Butler-Foucault-Williams argument"; that the idea of critique as suspension of judgment (or, in Melville's more abstract terms, as the ground of questioning) is "an extension of the bourgeois idea of aesthetic experience as essentially unconnected to necessity and instrumentality," which works by covertly replacing "the aesthetic with the critical."

Both these criticisms could move conversations on this topic forward. I have only one caveat: if Diederichsen had been present at the event that included Hickey and Melville, the pertinence of his arguments might not have been understood by some journalists who were also present, because it is couched in the language of dialectic philosophy. It is an academic argument, aimed at problems as they are framed in the academic community; but art criticism moves beyond those borders. If he had been at the event, Diederichsen might have started some interesting conversations with Melville and some others, but I can't imagine an extended conversation with Hickey or some journalist art critics who were also present. I do not mean that Diederichsen would not have been understood by Melville or some of the other academically minded critics who were present. I mean that the problem at hand goes beyond its framing within philosophic discourse. That's the problem I was aiming at with my initial question to Hickey and Melville: what would a conversation that bridged the different understandings of judgment look like? To me the gap between judgment and thought about judgment is wider than disagreements between Butler, say, and those who might want to reframe her politics. The problem is how to talk differently, to talk outside of the ordinary ground of conversation that takes "judgment" as a known term, even a philosopheme.

3. In regard to what exemplifies art criticism

One of the principal contemporary tendencies in criticism is what might be called performative criticism. By that I mean critical writing that is construed as performance, or as performative; it is intended to respond to new kinds of art that are themselves evanescent, body-centered, and time-based, such as performance art. Versions of this practice can be seen, for example, in the book *After Criticism.*[6] The central writer in this regard may be Irit Rogoff; her theory of the development of art criticism from criticism to critique to criticality is mentioned here by Tirdad Zolghadr. He says Rogoff's sequence "is of course easily parodied as affected and pompous." My difficulty with it is that I am not convinced that "criticality" has any coherent definition. In practice, Rogoff uses it to describe situations in which the critic's role, her purpose and voice, are so much at risk—so intimately engaged with the artist's work—that her subjectivity, and her practice, may alter, and in turn alter the reception of the work. I find it at once a hypertrophied description of any phenomenologically understood encounter with an artwork, unhelpfully ideal as a standard for interesting art, and—most important in this context— not cogent as a contribution to the historical lineage that produced the first two terms, criticism and critique. It answers neither Kant nor Hegel, and it does not persuasively alter the terms of critical discourse that depend on them.

Perhaps it is best to define criticism through practice

rather than against other traditions. Performative criticism makes use of a very wide range of rhetorical strategies in order to avoid the linear, logical, deductive argument that it associates with traditional criticism and its production of unambiguous judgment. (I say "it associates" because a study of older criticism shows just how performative it sometimes was. Diderot was far more performative at times than any contemporary critic I know. But what is at issue here is the self-description of contemporary critics.) Critics have been drawn to writers such as Hélène Cixous as models for such experimental writing.

In *Judgment and Contemporary Art Criticism*, some of these possibilities are beautifully articulated—and also embodied—by Maria Fusco. She writes, for example, that a critic might "induce" the artwork's "essential obscurity" by responding with "essential obscurity" and that criticism could be "a procedure of induction rather than deduction," which could help avoid the kind of writing whose purpose is "tracking a logical conclusion." She advocates "parlous…navigation" and a "backwards movement" of argument. This is attractive, and in the hands of writers such as Fusco, Cixous, or Jean-Louis Schefer, many kinds of nonlinear writing can be engaging and apparently appropriate for contemporary art practices. They become problematic only when they ask to be read as examples of art criticism, as working definitions of art criticism, or as responses to other people's positions about art criticism. I can read Fusco's essay only as an example of itself and its own concerns about writing and art. I can't read it as a way to frame an activity that it would make sense to call art criticism, because that activity has become sensible through different kinds of claims.

A related position is articulated by Lütticken who proposed, following Andrea Fraser, "site-specific criticism," meaning criticism rethought and remade for each individual occasion. This is also an excellent ideal, like Plagens's ideas of "wildness," and it has the added virtue of alertness to the logic of the work and the reciprocal logic of the critical text. I do not object to such ideals, but they are not, in themselves, either definitions or directions for art criticism, because they apply too broadly. What critic, Diderot included, would say he wasn't responding to the logic of the individual work?

The fact that the best and most successful contemporary experimental writing about art is only and entirely its own project poses a root-level challenge for any number of inventive contemporary practices if they are interested in retaining affinities to something called art criticism. I don't think it is possible to respond to such practices as responses to older or existing practices that are identified as art criticism. The new practices can be examples and models, but they are not part of the project of rethinking art criticism in particular. And this problem becomes only more difficult when we think of art criticism (as I'd like to do) as an aggregate of practices that includes not only serious experimental prose but the most superficial and abbreviated journalism and the most clearly commercial gallery brochures.

These three are fundamental issues (history, purpose, form), by which I mean they have the potential to disrupt one another and the entire project of art criticism. It helps to acknowledge that art criticism is not a well-defined field within which such problems can be discussed in a normative fashion. Art criticism is not a "normal" field in Thomas Kuhn's sense: its problems are not contained within its rhetoric but exist sometimes outside that rhetoric, with the potential of undermining the field itself. It would seem, given this situation, that there would be concerted efforts to comprehend the limits of the conceptualization of contemporary art criticism. But I find that such efforts are only scattered and intermittent. This suggests a fourth issue, a kind of meta-problem for art criticism.

4. Unaccountably, none of these three issues has provoked sustained interest

The practice, or practices, of art criticism are diverse, and that diversity does not often bother critics. At the end of the *The State of Art Criticism*, Michael Newman and I printed an exchange of letters on this subject. We were wondering how it was that so many contributors to the book did not engage the fundamental questions (including the three I have just named) that were raised at the beginning of the project. Why were so many art critics, from so many different backgrounds, uninterested in clarifying the history, purposes, and forms of their own practice? Almost every contributor in *The State of Art Criticism* noted the problem of judgment, for example, but hardly any thought it was worth pursuing. At the time it occurred to me that this could not happen in the sciences. Everyone involved in CERN (European Organization for Nuclear Research), for instance, presumably agrees on the gaps in the current conceptualization of subatomic particles (the question of the origin of mass, the nature of gravity, and so on). Even engineers and other technical specialists, whose work takes place far from the teams who work on the major experiments, presumably know about such issues and agree they are of fundamental importance. There is no such thing as a person who works on particle physics who simply doesn't care what happens with subatomic particles. Like many analogies between science and culture, this one is tricky and partly inappropriate, but I think it is exact enough to capture what is so strange about art criticism. Even in a field closer to art criticism, for example literary criticism, there is general agreement on the importance—if not the force, pertinence, or truth—of foundational thinking such as the poststructural critique associated with Paul De Man and others. Every serious academic literary critic will have come to terms with poststructuralism in some way, but in Newman's and my experience few critics care about even large conceptual inconsistencies in their own field.

This fourth issue is a second-order problem, an obstacle to working on the first three problems, and it is an obstacle that derives its objections from sources sometimes entirely outside the issues that drive those first three problems. In other words, many critics do not have considered positions on problems like the first three, and they do not possess accounts of why they do not require considered positions on those problems. Logically speaking, this creates a third-order problem: not having positions about fundamental problems itself comprises a second-order problem, and not having an account of why it is not necessary to have a position is a third-order problem. The fifth and last issue I want to raise is also a second- or third-order problem, but it is easier to state.

*5. People do not read the literature on art criticism,
so writers often repeat texts and ideas that have
already been articulated*

This is the main reason I am not planning on keeping up with the literature: I find it frustrating that the same issues get raised over and over, and that the people who raise them are unaware that their ideas have been formulated by others. They therefore miss opportunities to build discourse by critiquing or strengthening previous positions. In the Vancouver forum, a number of issues repeat debates already articulated in Adorno and the literature that follows him, especially Jay Bernstein; and there are discussions in more recent publications that could have provided stronger starting points for ideas the speakers raise. I wonder, again, if this kind of situation could happen in the sciences. At the least, the rediscovery of ideas that are already in the literature prevents discourse on art criticism from building into a common conversation: something that many critics, including some as different as Sarat Maharaj, Boris Groys, and Jean Fisher, have said they would like. It probably isn't possible to make this point without sounding overbearing, but it does matter, because if there is not a common core of texts (as there is, for example, in visual studies, which circles around Foucault, Benjamin, Lacan, and a few others), then conferences and books on art criticism will tend to be mostly made of old ideas, inaccurately repeated from unknown sources. And that would create a crisis in any field.

There is another way to look at all this. Perhaps the irresolutions of these five issues are symptoms of the current state of affairs and not problems to be solved: it's entirely possible that these are conventional limits to our discourse and that the best thing to do is describe them, not solve them—to increase our awareness of them, along with our awareness of why we do not want to work directly on them. It feels that way to me, but it also seems clear that some very interesting discussions are waiting to take place around problems like these.

1. *The 4th International Conference of the Novo Nordisk Foundation Art History Project*, Copenhagen, February 26–March 1, 2009.

2. *Posibilidad, unutilidad, y acción: Entre la accademia y el periodismo*, Universidad de los Andes, Bogotà, Colombia, October 6–8, 2008.

3. The 2nd China Contemporary Art Forum, *What Happened to Art Criticism?—Problems in Chinese and Western Art Criticism*, The Central Academy of Fine Art, Beijing, May 19–22, 2010.

4. *The State of Art Criticism*, co-edited with Michael Newman (New York: Routledge, 2007) is part of a series called *The Art Seminar* (New York: Routledge, 2005–08, 7 vols.). At the end of the last volume of that series, called *Re-Enchantment*, co-edited by David Morgan, vol. 7 of *The Art Seminar* (New York: Routledge, 2008), I wrote an "envoi" looking back over the books in the series. Each book was on a different subject, and each revealed a different kind of incoherence or unity. This paragraph is adapted from that "envoi."

5. This is a charge Peter Plagens made in an e-mail, responding to the pamphlet *What Happened to Art Criticism?* (2004). His criticism at the time was that academic writers have ruined the criticism of theatre, music, and other subjects, and that art criticism remains one of the few refuges for "wild" writing.

6. *After Criticism: New Responses to Art and Performance*, ed. Gavin Butt (Malden, Mass.: Blackwell, 2005).

A Crime Against Art, DVD. Directed by Hila Peleg. Paris: BDV, 2007.

Adorno, Theodor. *Aesthetic Theory*. Minneapolis: University of Minnesota Press, 1996.

Alberro, Alexander. *Conceptual Art: A Critical Anthology*. Cambridge, Mass.: The MIT Press, 2000.

Alloway, Lawrence. "The Function of the Art Critic." *New York University Education Quarterly 2* (1974), 24–28.

Art Criticism in the Sixties. New York: October House, 1967.

Berger, Maurice. *The Crisis of Criticism*. New York: The New Press, 1998.

Berman, Art. *From the New Criticism to Deconstruction: The Reception of Structuralism and Post-Structuralism*. Chicago: University of Illinois Press, 1988.

Birnbaum, Daniel and Isabelle Graw, eds. *The Power of Judgment: A Debate on Aesthetic Critique*. Berlin: Sternberg Press, 2010.

Bishop, Claire. *Participation*. Cambridge, Mass.: The MIT Press, 2006.

Bourriaud, Nicolas. *Relational Aesthetics*. Dijon: Les Presses du réel, 1998.

Bovier, Lionel, ed. *Liam Gillick: Proxemics, Selected Essays, 1988–2006*. Zurich: JRP Ringier, 2006.

Bois, Yve-Alain, Benjamin H. D. Buchloh, Denis Hollier, Silvia Kolbowski, Rosalind Krauss, and Annette Michelson. *October: The Second Decade, 1986–1996*. Cambridge, Mass.: The MIT Press, 1997.

Buchloh, Benjamin, Hal Foster, Andrea Fraser, David Joselit, Rosalind Krauss, et al, "Round Table: The Present Conditions of Art Criticism," *October* no. 100 (spring 2002).

Butler, Judith, "What Is Critique? An Essay on Foucault's Virtue," in David Ingram, ed., *The Political: Readings in Continental Philosophy*. London: Basil Blackwell, 2002.

Byvanck, Valentijn, ed. *Conventions in Contemporary Art: Lectures and Debates Witte de With 2001*. Rotterdam: Witte de With, Center for Contemporary Art, 2002.

Carrier, David. *Rosalind Krauss American Philosophical Art Criticism: From Formalism to Beyond Postmodernism*. Westport, Conn.: Praeger, 2002.

Copjec, Joan, Douglas Crimp, Rosalind Krauss, and Annette Michelson, eds. *October: The First Decade*. Cambridge, Mass.: The MIT Press, 1988.

Crow, Thomas. *Modern Art in the Common Culture*. New Haven: Yale University Press, 1998.

Crow, Thomas. *The Intelligence of Art*. Chapel Hill: The University of North Carolina Press, 2000.

Culler, Jonathan. *Literary Theory: A Very Short Introduction*. New York: Oxford University Press, 2000.

Culler, Jonathan. *On Deconstruction: Theory and Criticism After Structuralism*. Ithaca: Cornell University Press, 1983.

Danto, Arthur C. *The Transfiguration of the Commonplace*. Cambridge, Mass.: Harvard University Press, 1981.

Darrieussecq, Marie. *White.* London: Faber and Faber, 2005.

Davila, Thierry. *Geoffrey Farmer-Sourcebook.* Rotterdam: Witte de With, Center for Contemporary Art, 2008.

Deepwell, Katy. *Art Criticism and Africa.* London: Saffron, 1997.

De Man, Paul. *Aesthetic Ideology.* Minneapolis: University of Minnesota Press, 1996.

De Man, Paul. *The Resistance to Theory.* Minneapolis: University of Minnesota Press, 1986.

De Man, Paul. *Blindness and Insight: Essays on the Rhetoric of Contemporary Criticism.* Minneapolis: University of Minnesota Press, 1983.

Denison, Roger, and Thomas McEvilley. *Capacity: History, the World, and the Self in Contemporary Art and Criticism.* Amsterdam: G & B Arts, 1996.

Derksen, Jeff. *After Euphoria: art/space/neoliberalism.* Vancouver: ECU Press, 2010.

Diederichsen, Diedrich. *Argument Son.* Zurich: JRP Ringier, 2007.

Diederichsen, Diedrich. *On (Surplus) Value in Art.* Berlin: Sternberg Press, 2008.

Drucker, Joanna. *Sweet Dreams: Contemporary Art and Complicity.* Chicago: University of Chicago Press, 2005.

Eagleton, Terry. *The Function of Criticism.* London: Verso, 1984.

Elkins, James. *What Happened to Art Criticism?* Chicago: Prickly Paradigm Press, 2003.

Elkins, James and Michael Newman, eds. *The State of Art Criticism.* New York: Routledge, 2008.

Elkins, James. *Is Art History Global?* New York: Routledge, 2006.

Esche, Charles. *Art and Social Change: A Critical Reader.* London: Tate, 2008.

Everett, Sally, ed. *Art Theory and Criticism: An Anthology of Formalist, Avant-Garde, Contextualist, and Post-Modernist Thought.* Jefferson, NC: McFarland, 1995.

Feldman, Edmund Burke. *Practical Art Criticism.* Upper Saddle River, NJ: Prentice Hall, 1994.

Foster, Hal. *The Return of the Real: Art and Theory at the End of the Century.* Cambridge, Mass.: The MIT Press, 1996.

Foucault, Michel. *The Archaeology of Knowledge and the Discourse on Language.* New York: Routledge, 1997.

Fried, Michael. *Art and Objecthood: Essays and Reviews.* Chicago: University of Chicago Press, 1998.

Fusco, Maria, ed. *Put About: A Critical Anthology on Independent Publishing.* London: Book Works, 2004.

Gage, John, ed. *Goethe on Art.* Berkeley: University of California Press, 1980.

Greenberg, Clement. *The Collected Essays and Criticism*. Volume 1, *Perceptions and Judgments, 1939–1944*. Ed. John O'Brian. Chicago: University of Chicago Press, 1988.

Greenberg, Clement. *The Collected Essays and Criticism*. Volume 2, *Arrogant Purpose, 1945–1949*. Ed. John O'Brian. Chicago: University of Chicago Press, 1988.

Greenberg, Clement. *The Collected Essays and Criticism*. Volume 3, *Affirmations and Refusals, 1950–1956*. Ed. John O'Brian. Chicago: University of Chicago Press, 1995.

Greenberg, Clement. *The Collected Essays and Criticism*. Volume 4, *Modernism with a Vengeance, 1957–1969*. Ed. John O'Brian. Chicago: University of Chicago Press, 1995.

Gronlund, Melissa, ed. *Frieze Projects: Artists' Commissions and Talks*. New York: Frieze, 2006.

Groys, Boris. *Art Power*. Cambridge, Mass.: The MIT Press, 2008.

Groys, Boris in Conversation with Brian Dillon. "Who do you think you're talking to?" *frieze* no. 121 (March 2009), 126–31.

Guilbaut, Serge. *How New York Stole the Idea of Modern Art*. Chicago: University of Chicago Press, 1985.

Harari, Josue V. *Textual Strategies: Perspectives in Post-Structuralist Criticism*. London: Methuen, 1980.

Harrison, Charles, ed. *Art in Theory: 1815–1900*. Oxford: Wiley-Blackwell, 1998.

Harrison, Charles, ed. *Art in Theory: 1900–2000*. Oxford: Wiley-Blackwell, 2002.

Hegel, G. W. F. *Hegel's Aesthetics: Lectures on Fine Art*, trans. T. M. Knox. Oxford: Clarendon, 1975.

Heiser, Jorg. *All of a Sudden*. Berlin: Sternberg Press, 2008.

Hlavajova, Maria, Jill Winder, and Binna Choi. *On Knowledge Production: A Critical Reader in Contemporary Art*. Utrecht: BAK, 2008.

Hume, David. *Selected Essays*. New York: Oxford University Press, 1996.

Irwin, David, ed. *Winckelmann: Writings on Art*. London: Phaidon, 1972.

Judd, Donald. *Complete Writings 1959–75*. New York: New York University Press, 1975.

Kant, Immanuel. *Critique of the Power of Judgment*. Cambridge: Cambridge University Press, 2001.

Kant, Immanuel. *Observations on the Feeling of the Beautiful and Sublime*. Trans. John T. Goldthwait. Berkeley: University of California Press, 1961.

Keller, Christoph and Michael Laliach, eds. *Kiosk: Modes of Multiplication*. Zurich: JRP Ringier, 2009.

Kester, Grant. *Conversation Pieces: Community and Communication in Modern Art*. Berkeley: University of California Press, 2004.

Kingston, Angela. *Hygiene: Writers and Artists Come Clean and Talk Dirty*. Birmingham: Ikon Gallery, 1994.

Kokoli, Alexandra, ed. *Susan Hiller: The Provisional Texture of Reality, Selected Talks and Texts, 1977–2007.* Zurich: JRP Ringier and Les Presses du réel, 2008.

Kotz, Liz. *Words To Be Looked Art: Language in the 1960s Art.* Cambridge, Mass.: The MIT Press, 2007.

Krauss, Rosalind E. *The Originality of the Avant-Garde and Other Myths.* Cambridge, Mass.: The MIT Press, 1985.

Kuspit, Donald. *Dialectic of Decadence: Between Advance and Decline in Art.* New York: Allworth Press, 2000.

Kwon, Miwon. *One Place after Another: Site-Specific Art and Locational Identity.* Cambridge, Mass.: The MIT Press, 2004.

Langer, Cassandra. *Feminist Art Criticism: An Annotated Bibliography.* New York: G. K. Hall, 1993.

Lentricchia, Frank. *After the New Criticism.* Chicago: University of Chicago Press, 1980.

Lewitt, Sol. *0 to 9 (Lost Literature).* New York: Ugly Duckling Presse, 2006.

Lippard, Lucy. *Changing: Essays in Art Criticism.* New York: E. P. Dutton, 1971.

Lippard, Lucy. *Six Years: The Dematerialization of the Art Object from 1966 to 1972.* Chicago: University of Chicago Press, 1997.

Lütticken, Sven. *Secret Publicity: Essays on Contemporary Culture.* Rotterdam: NAi Publishers, 2006.

Lyotard, Jean-Francois. *The Postmodern Condition: A Report on Knowledge.* Minneapolis: University of Minnesota Press, 1984.

Martin, Jean-Hubert. *Cautionary Tales: Critical Curating.* New York: apexart, 2007.

Miller, Earl. "The State of Art Criticism and Critical Theory," *C Magazine* no. 100 (winter 2009), 35–37.

Miller, John. *The Price Club: Selected Writings (1977–1998).* Geneva and Dijon: JRP Editions and Les Presses du réel.

Newman, Amy. *Challenging Art: Artforum 1962–1974.* New York: Soho Press, 2000.

Obrist, Hans Ulrich, ed. *A Brief History of Curating.* Zurich: JRP Ringier and Les Presses du réel. 2008.

Rancière, Jacques. *The Politics of Aesthetics.* New York: Continuum, 2004.

Raunig, Gerald. *Art and Revolution: Transversal Activism in the Long Twentieth Century.* Cambridge, Mass.: The MIT Press, 2007.

Raven, Arlene. *Art in the Public Interest.* Cambridge, Mass.: Da Capo Press, 1993.

Rogoff, Irit. "What is a Theorist?" In *Was Ist ein Kuenstler?* Eds. Katharyna Sykora et al. Munich: Wilhelm Fink, 2004.

Rubinstein, Raphael. *Critical Mess: Art Critics on the State of their Practice.* Lenox, Mass.: Hard Press Editions, 2006.

Sholis, Brian. "Reinventing Criticism." *Fillip* no. 6 (summer 2007), 28.

Smagula, Howard J. *Revisions: New Perspectives of Art Criticism.* Upper Saddle River, NJ: Prentice Hall, 1990.

Smithson, Robert. *Robert Smithson: The Collected Writings.* New York: New York University Press, 1979.

Snyder, Sean, ed. *e-flux journal reader 2009.* New York: Sternberg Press, 2009.

Sontag, Susan. *Against Interpretation and Other Essays.* New York: Picador, 1990.

Stallabrass, Julian. *Art Incorporated: The Story of Contemporary Art.* New York: Oxford University Press, 2004.

Stimson, Blake. *Collectivism after Modernism: The Art of Social Imagination after 1945.* Minneapolis: University of Minnesota Press, 2007.

Velthuis, Olav. *Talking Prices: Symbolic Meanings of Prices on the Market for Contemporary Art.* Princeton: Princeton University Press, 2005.

Venturi, Lionello. *Art Criticism Now.* Baltimore: The Johns Hopkins Press, 1964.

Venturi, Lionello. *History of Art Criticism.* New York: E. P. Dutton, 1964.

Winckelmann, Johann Joachim. "A Treatise on the Ability to Per-ceive the Beautiful in Art and Instruction in the Same." In Denis Marshall Sweet, *Winckelmann's Writings on Art: An Introduction to Classicist Aesthetics in Eighteenth-Century Germany,* Ph.D. diss., Stanford University, 1978.

Jeff Derksen is a cultural critic and poet who teaches at Simon Fraser University. His writing on art and culture has appeared in *Springerin, Hunch, C Magazine,* and *Open Letter,* among other publications. He is the author of *Annihilated Time: Poetry and Other Politics* (Talonbooks, 2009) and *After Euphoria: art/space/neoliberalism* (ECU Press and JRP Ringier, forthcoming). Derksen was a research fellow at the Center for Place, Culture, and Politics, CUNY Graduate Centre, New York, and is a founding member of the Kootenay School of Writing. Under the name Urban Subjects, he collaborates with Sabine Bitter and Helmut Weber on curatorial projects and visual research.

Diedrich Diederichsen was editor of several music magazines in the 1980s (including *Sounds*, Hamburg, and *Spex*, Cologne) and has taught at academies in Germany, Austria, and the US in the fields of art history, musicology, theatre studies, and cultural studies. He is Professor for Theory, Practice and Communication of Contemporary Art at the Academy of Fine Art, Vienna. His writing is seen regularly in art and culture publications such as the magazines *Texte zur Kunst, Fillip, Artforum,* and *Die Zeit*, and in newspapers such as *Tagesspiegel* and *Tageszeitung*. Recent publications include *Eigenblutdoping* (Kiepenheuer und Witsch, 2008), *Kritik des Auges* (Philo Fine Arts, 2008), *Argument Son* (JRP Ringier, 2007), and *Personas en loop* (Stockcero, 2005).

James Elkins is an art historian and art critic. He teaches art history, theory, and criticism at the School of the Art Institute of Chicago. He is the author of *What Happened to Art Criticism?* (Prickly Paradigm Press, 2003) and *Artists with PhDs: On the New Doctoral Degree in Studio Art* (New Academia Publishing, 2009).

Maria Fusco is a Belfast-born writer and academic based in London. She is a regular contributor to international books, catalogues, and magazines and is Director of Art Writing in the Department of Art at Goldsmiths, University of London. She commissioned and edited *Put About: A Critical Anthology on Independent Publishing* (Book Works) and convened an accompanying symposium in collaboration with Tate Modern in 2004; she is also founding editor of the *Happy Hypocrite,* a biannual journal for and about experimental art writing. In 2008–09 she was Critic-in-Residence at Kadist Art Foundation, Paris, and is the inaugural Writer-in-Residence at Whitechapel Gallery, London.

Jeff Khonsary is a Vancouver-based publisher, curator, and designer. Recent curatorial projects include *Motto Storefront* (Artspeak, 2010), *Copy Room* (Langara College Centre for Art in Public Space, 2009), and *Ear to Ear* (Or Gallery/Cornershop Projects, 2008). Currently, he is Co-Director of Fillip Editions and Publisher of *Fillip* magazine. With Courtenay Webber, he is a co-founder of The Future, a Vancouver-based design studio.

Sven Lütticken is a Netherlands-based critic and historian. A regular contributor to catalogues and art magazines such as *Artforum, New Left Review, Afterimage,* and *Texte zur Kunst,* he is the author of *Secret Publicity: Essays on Contemporary Art* (2006) and *Idols of the Market: Modern Iconoclasm and the Fundamentalist Spectacle* (2009). He teaches art history at VU University Amsterdam.

Tom Morton is a critic and curator based in London. He is a curator at the Hayward Gallery, where he has organized exhibitions by Cyprien Gaillard, Guido van der Werve, and Matthew Darbyshire. In October 2010, he will co-curate the major traveling exhibition *British Art Show 7*. He was previously curator at Cubitt Gallery, London, and co-curator of the 2008 Busan Biennale. Morton has been contributing editor of *frieze* since 2003 and also writes regularly for *Bidoun* and *GQ Style*. He has written numerous exhibition catalogue essays, including on artists Roger Hiorns, Erik van Lieshout, Pierre Huyghe, Glenn Brown, Andro Wekua, and Victor Man.

John O'Brian is Professor of Art History and Brenda and David McLean Chair at the University of British Columbia, Vancouver. His books include *Beyond Wilderness: The Group of Seven, Canadian Identity, and Contemporary Art* (McGill-Queen's University Press, 2007), *Ruthless Hedonism: The American Reception of Matisse* (University of Chicago Press, 1998), *Clement Greenberg: The Collected Essays and Criticism* (University of Chicago Press, 1986–93), and *David Milne and the Modern Tradition of Painting* (Coach House Press, 1983). His current research is on the engagement of photography with the atomic era.

Melanie O'Brian is Director/Curator at Artspeak. She has written for *Yishu*, *Border Crossings*, *Mix*, *C Magazine*, *Last Call,* and *Fillip*, and recently contributed catalogue essays for *Damian Moppett* (Carleton University Art Gallery, 2007) and *The Décor Project* (Projectile Publishing, 2007). She is the editor of *Vancouver Art and Economies* (Arsenal Pulp Press and Artspeak, 2007).

Kristina Lee Podesva is a Vancouver-based artist, writer, and editor of *Fillip*. She is the founder of colourschool, a free school within a school dedicated to the speculative and collaborative study of five colours (white, black, red, yellow, and brown), and the co-founder of Cornershop Projects, a programmatic framework for exploring the relationship between art and economic exchange.

Jordan Strom is a curator and writer based in Vancouver. He is Founding Editor of *Fillip*. He currently works as Curator of Exhibitions and Collections at the Surrey Art Gallery.

William Wood is an art historian and critic. Since 1984, he has published on recent art in journals, anthologies, and exhibition catalogues, as well as held editorial positions with *C Magazine*, *Public*, *Vanguard*, and *Parachute*. Recent catalogue essays and articles have dealt with artists such as Stan Douglas, Brian Jungen, Mike Kelley, Becky Singleton, and the entity known as the Vancouver School. He has taught art history and critical theory at universities in Canada and the United Kingdom.

Tirdad Zolghadr is an independent writer and curator based in Berlin. He writes for *frieze* and teaches at the Center for Curatorial Studies, Bard College, New York. Zolghadr is currently curating the Taipei Biennial 2010 with Hongjohn Lin. He recently organized the UAE (United Arab Emirates) pavilion at the Venice Biennale 2009 and the long-term exhibition project *Lapdogs of the Bourgeoisie,* with Nav Haq. Zolghadr is editor-at-large for *Cabinet*. His first novel, *Softcore*, was published by Telegram Books in 2007. The working title of his second novel is *Top Ten*.

Colophon

Judgment and Contemporary Art Criticism
Published by Artspeak and Fillip Editions
Fillip Folio Series: A
Design: The Future
Printed in Belgium by Die Keure

© 2010 by Artspeak, Fillip, and the authors. All rights reserved. No part of this book may be reproduced in any manner without permission in writing by the publishers.

Fillip's Folio Series presents anthologies of new and previously published writing by critics, artists, and curators that engages specific and recurring questions on international contemporary art.

Library and Archives Canada
Cataloguing in Publication

Judgment and contemporary art criticism / authors: Diedrich Diederichsen... [et al.] ; edited by: Jeff Khonsary, Melanie O'Brian.

(Folio series ; A)
Co-published by: Artspeak.
Based on papers presented at the Judgment and Contemporary Art Criticism conference held in Vancouver, BC, on Feb. 27–28, 2009.
Includes bibliographical references.
ISBN 978-0-9738133-6-4

1. Art criticism. 2. Judgment (Aesthetics). 3. Art, Modern—21st century.
I. Diederichsen, Diedrich II. Khonsary, Jeff, 1979– III. O'Brian, Melanie, 1973– IV. Artspeak Gallery V. Series: Folio series A
N7475.J83 2010   701.18   C2010-900484-1

Artspeak
233 Carrall Street
Vancouver, BC
Canada V6B 2J2
www.artspeak.ca

Fillip Editions
305 Cambie Street
Vancouver, BC
Canada V6B 2N4
www.fillip.ca